Landscapes of
LANZAROTE

a countryside guide
Second edition

Noel Rochford

SUNFLOWER
BOOKS

Dedicated to Augustín Pallarés Padilla

Revised printing 2000
First published 1998
by Sunflower Books™
12 Kendrick Mews
London SW7 3HG, UK

Copyright © 1998
Sunflower Books.
All rights reserved.
No part of this publication
may be reproduced, stored
in a retrieval system, or
transmitted by any form
or by any means,
electronic, mechanical,
photocopying, recording
or otherwise, without the
prior written permission
of the publishers.
Sunflower Books and
'Landscapes' are
Registered Trademarks.

ISBN 1-85691-100-4

Timanfaya camel train

Important note to the reader ⎯⎯⎯⎯

We have tried to ensure that the descriptions and maps in this book are error-free at press date. The book will be updated, where necessary, whenever future printings permit. It will be very helpful for us to receive your comments (sent in care of the publishers, please) for the updating of future printings.

   We also rely on those who use this book — especially walkers — to take along a good supply of common sense when they explore. Conditions change fairly rapidly on Lanzarote, and **storm damage or bulldozing may make a route unsafe at any time**. If the route is not as we outline it here, and your way ahead is not secure, return to the point of departure. **Never attempt to complete a tour or walk under hazardous conditions!** Please read carefully the notes on pages 18 and 45-49, as well as the introductory comments at the beginning of each tour and walk (regarding road conditions, equipment, grade, distances and time, etc). Explore **safely**, while at the same time respecting the beauty of the countryside.

Cover photograph: view to La Graciosa from above Guinate (Walk 4)
Title page: old farmhouse at Haría (Walk 5)

Photographs pages 2, 13, 15 (bottom), 22, 23, 31, 51, 55, 58, 60, 70, 78, 79 (top), 80-81, 84, 85, 96, 118 (bottom), 121: the author; page 61: Reinhard Baumgärtner; page 109: David Young; all other photographs: John Underwood
Maps and plans: John Underwood
A CIP catalogue record for this book is available from the British Library.
Printed and bound in the UK by Brightsea Press, Exeter

10 9 8 7 6 5 4

 Contents

4 Landscapes of Lanzarote

The Monumento al Campesino (Car tour 2)

 Preface

Within just a few years, Lanzarote grew from a quiet, relatively unknown tourist resort to an island buzzing with a million tourists annually. Fortunately, these visitors are confined to three fairly small areas, and the rest of the island remains blissfully rural and unspoilt.

Few holidaymakers realise that Lanzarote has more to offer than just beaches and sunshine. I was sceptical. When my publisher suggested Lanzarote for my next book, I felt sure that I was doing penance for past manuscripts. But a pleasant surprise awaited me.

This fascinating 797-square-kilometre island is truly extraordinary. Its fate was decided over two and one-half centuries ago, when the largest volcanic eruption in recorded history took place, leaving a strange and alluring countryside in its wake — a landscape littered with volcanoes and dark streams of jagged lava. This is the backdrop to nearly every scene on the island, and intriguing sights abound, as you can see from the photographs in this book.

If you were to suggest walking on Lanzarote to most visitors, they would think you mad. 'Where is there to walk?' But I can think of no better place in the Canary Islands for just strolling. No doubt 'serious' walkers will find Tenerife, La Palma and Gran Canaria, for example, more challenging, but ramblers will be in their element on Lanzarote. Each of the walks in this book takes you to a different corner of the island and shows you a scenically-different outlook. But if walking is not your favourite pastime, then *do* rent a vehicle of sorts and explore on wheels. Use the book to reach places off the beaten track and see another face of Lanzarote.

When I wrote the first edition of this book in 1989, all eyes were on this island. Would it indeed set an example in preservation, or would it follow in the footsteps of Tenerife and Gran Canaria, falling prey to the concrete of greedy developers? Fortunately, Lanzarote had one advantage over the other islands. It was the home of the well-known artist-designer — and, more importantly, conservationist — the late César Manrique. Together with his supporters, he worked to preserve the island's environmental heritage. Despite the tourist boom of the

1980s, they succeeded in orchestrating a well-pitched harmony between man and the landscape. As a result, in 1994 Lanzarote was declared a 'World Reserve of the Biosphere' by UNESCO — the first such award ever given to an entire island.

I hope that *Landscapes of Lanzarote* convinces you that there is much more to the island than beaches and sunshine.

Acknowledgements

My thanks to the following people on Lanzarote, who helped me with the preparation of the first edition: Señor Francisco Ortega, Director, Patronato Insular de Turismo de Lanzarote; the Servicio Geográfico del Ejercito, Madrid, for permission to adapt their maps; Señores Carlos Gutierrez Gutierrez and Norberto Palomino Gallego, for additional military maps; ICONA; Jackie, for her errands; and very special thanks to Augustín Pallarés Padilla for invaluable suggestions and for hours spent answering my questions.

For the revision of this second edition my thanks to my publishers, John and Pat Underwood, and to Thea and Tiny Whitworth, David Young, and Reinhard Baumgärtner, who supplied notes for the new walks.

Finally, thanks to my family and friends, who always support my work and travels.

Useful books

Bramwell, D and Bramwell, Z: *Wild Flowers of the Canary Islands.* Stanley Thornes Ltd.

Bramwell, D and Bramwell, Z: *Historia Natural de las Islas Canarias.* Editorial Rueda; available in bookshops on the island.

Araña, Vicente and Carracedo, Juan: *Los volcanes de las Islas Canarias, II: Lanzarote y Fuerteventura* (with English text). Editorial Rueda; available in bookshops on the island.

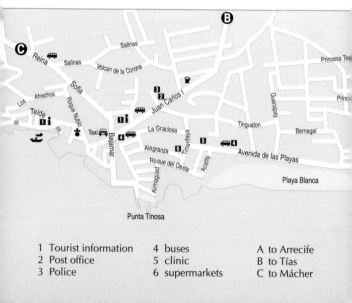

1 Tourist information	4 buses	A to Arrecife
2 Post office	5 clinic	B to Tías
3 Police	6 supermarkets	C to Mácher

❀ Getting about

The best way to get around Lanzarote is by **hired car**. This can be very economical, especially when you hire a car for a few days or a week. **Taxis** are only economical if shared, and all fares should be ascertained in advance. *Note:* never leave anything of value in your car. Lock your belongings in the boot, or carry them with you. Thefts from cars are not uncommon. Try, when possible, to park where there are other cars and people are about.

Coach tours are easy to arrange and get you to all the tourist points of interest, but never off the beaten track. The **local bus service** is very limited outside Puerto del Carmen and Costa Teguise; it serves the school children and villagers. Most of the walks in this book *can* be reached by local bus, however — with departures from Arrecife. Bus timetables are shown on pages 122-125. Don't rely *solely* on these, however. As soon as you arrive on the island, update these timetables by getting 'first-hand' information from the *bus station* or the local newspaper, *La Voz* (it's best *not* to rely on tourist office handouts). See town plans below and on pages 8 and 9 *for bus stops and stations.* Although buses may sometimes run late, you should *always arrive about fifteen minutes early.* In the Arrecife bus station it will take you that long just to find your bus!

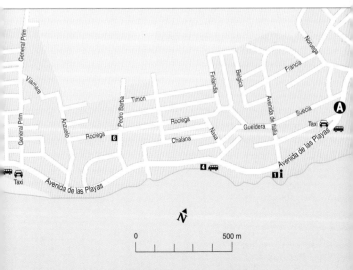

0   500 m

PUERTO DEL CARMEN

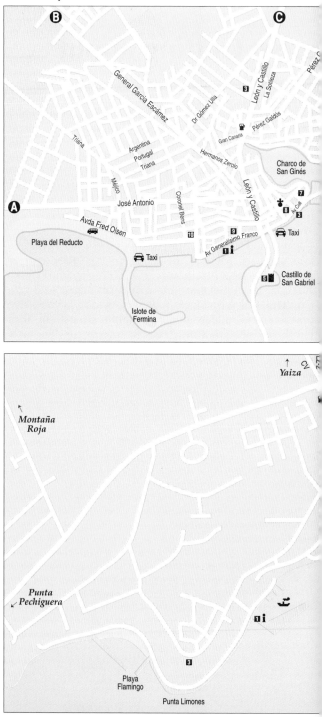

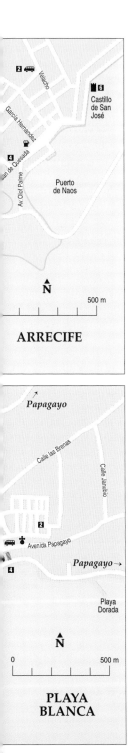

ARRECIFE

1 Tourist information
2 Bus station
3 Police
4 Hospital
5 Archaeological museum
   (Castillo de San Gabriel)
6 Art gallery (Castillo de
   San José)
7 Town hall
8 Fish market
9 Post office
10 Clinic

City exits
A   to the airport and
    Puerto del Carmen
B   to Tinajo
C   to Teguise
D   to the port

PLAYA BLANCA

1 Tourist information; also
   ferry ticket offices
   (ferries to Corralejo,
   Puerto del Carmen, Lobos)
2 Post office
3 Clinic
4 Waterside promenade with
   shops and restaurants

 Picnicking

Picnicking isn't one of Lanzarote's strong points. Shade is the biggest problem — there are not many trees on the island! Nor are there any 'organised' picnic sites, as there are on other Canary Islands — unless you count the few tables at El Bosquecillo.

Nevertheless, there *are* many lovely picnic spots — if you know where to look! Throughout the car tours I call your attention to both *roadside* picnic spots (most of them in shade) and the more remote settings you can reach during a fairly short walk. On the following pages I tell you more about these off-the-beaten-track locations, which I've come upon when out walking. Note that picnic numbers correspond to walk numbers; thus you can quickly find the general location on the island by referring to the pull-out touring map (where the walks are outlined in green). Most of the spots I've chosen are very easy to reach, and I outline transport details (🚌: bus information; 🚗: where to park if you're travelling by car), walking times, and views or setting. Beside the picnic title, you'll also find a map reference: the *precise* location of the picnic spot is shown on the relevant large-scale

walking map by the symbol *P*. Some of the picnic settings are also illustrated; if so, a photograph reference follows the map reference.

If you have just one day for picnicking, don't miss Picnic 2 (Risco de Famara). I think this is one of the loveliest and most memorable places to enjoy a picnic in the entire archipelago.

Please glance over the comments before you start off on your picnic: if some walking is involved, remember to wear sensible shoes and to take a sunhat (○ = picnic in full sun). It's a good idea to take along a plastic sheet as well, in case the ground is damp.

If you are travelling to your picnic by bus, be sure to verify departure times in advance. Although there are timetables in this book, they do change from time to time, without prior warning. **If you are travelling to your picnic by car**, *never* block a road or track when you park.

All picnickers should read the country code on page 18 and go quietly in the countryside. *Buen provecho!*

Picnic suggestions

1 LA GRACIOSA (map page 53) ○

by 🛥: 20-25min on foot. Ferry from Orzola to La Graciosa
Off the ferry, skirt the waterfront, heading west, and continue around in front of and through the houses on the shore. Beyond the houses you come to a superb beach and shortly after, a tidal lagoon. It's a fantastic spot, from where you look across to the Risco de Famara.

2 RISCO DE FAMARA (map pages 56-57, photograph page 15, bottom) ○

by 🚗 only: 5-10min on foot. Park by the side of the track, 2.4km southwest of the Mirador del Río: descending from the *mirador* as in Car tour 1, watch for two derelict stone buildings set just below the side of the road. A dyke (a natural wall of rock) cuts across to the right directly behind them and, immediately beyond it, a track forks off right into the fields (alongside the dyke). Turn off onto the track and follow it to the end — or, if the track is too rough, park alongside the buildings.

El Golfo is a fine spot for a picnic. While there are many tourists coming and going, they don't stay very long — and some don't even explore as far as this cloudy green lagoon, the Charco de los Clicos. The crater walls provide ample shade.

View from the Pico de las Nieves (Picnic 6a)

Sit on the ledge of the cliff, below the track, and overlook the Mirador del Río vista — now you'll have the view all to yourself. No other picnic spot on the island matches this one. Cliffs provide the only shade.

3 MAGUEZ (map pages 56-57, photograph pages 61-61) ○

by 🚌: 40min on foot. Bus to Máguez and follow Walk 3.
by 🚗: 25min on foot. On entering Máguez *from the north,* you en-counter a fork in the road: bear left and, a few hundred metres/yards along, you will see a track cutting back sharply to the left. Park at the side of the road here, without obstructing traffic.
Set off along the track and picnic anywhere you like. My favourite spot is just beyond the intersection at the 35min-point (page 60). Here you can picnic on a grassy hillock, with a lovely view over cultivated slopes down to the east coast, and Monte Corona standing just behind you.

4 LOS HELECHOS (map pages 56-57, photograph page 64) ○

by 🚗 only: 5-35min on foot. Park below Los Helechos (see the notes for Short walk 4 on page 62).
There are many places to picnic on grassy slopes — at the edge of the plateau (5min), by the white building (10min), from where you look down to a farm and the Risco cliffs and La Graciosa, or at the trig point (35min). Some shade at the white building.

5a OVERLOOKING HARIA (map pages 56-57, nearby photograph pages 15, 68-69) ○

by 🚌 and 🚗 taxi: 1h on foot. Do Short walk 5-1 (page 66).
by 🚗: 10-20min on foot. Park at the Restaurante Los Helechos (with *mirador*) on the LZ10 above Haría. Follow Short walk 5-1 (page 66) for as long as you like.
The setting is a flower-filled old pilgrims' trail, from where you have wonderful views down the Valle de Malpaso and over Haría.

5b VALLE DE LOS CASTILLEJOS (map pages 56-57, photograph page 18) ○

by 🚌 or 🚗 to Haría: 20min on foot.
Follow Short walk 5-2 (page 66) for as long as you like; there are lovely views over cultivation and to Máguez after about 10min.

6a ERMITA DE LAS NIEVES (map pages 72-73, photograph opposite) ○

by 🚗 only: up to 5min on foot. Park by the Ermita de las Nieves, off the LZ10.
Picnic anywhere on the top of the crest. The views across the centre of Lanzarote and out to its neighbouring islands are magnificent. There is some shade from the chapel walls.

6b ERMITA DE SAN JOSE (map page 72-73) ○

by 🚗 only: no walking. Park by the chapel ruins, off the LZ10 outside Teguise. These large honey-coloured ruins are opposite the Castillo de Santa Bárbara and are easily seen from the road. Use the large-scale map on pages 72-73 to drive there.
These old ruins are picturesque and provide some shade. They are encountered near the end of Walk 6.

8 MONTAÑA DE GUARDILAMA (map pages 82-83, photograph page 84) ○

by 🚌: 1h on foot. Bus to Uga and follow Walk 8.
by 🚗: up to 45min on foot. Turn off the LZ30 (La Geria road) 600m/yds past the junction north of Uga (just past the km22 stone), onto the first track forking off east. Park off the side of the road at the entrance to the

Playa de Papa-gayo (Picnic 11). If you enjoy some sand in your sarnies, then this is the most beautiful setting on the island for a picnic on the beach.

track; don't block the track. If you travel by jeep, you can drive up to the pass below Guardilama.

Use the notes on pages 81-82 to reach the pass, or go only as far as you wish up the track. You have a superb view over the dark Geria Valley — quite a sight when the vines are coming into leaf (see photographs pages 28-29 and 80-81).

9 ATALAYA DE FEMES (map page 88, photographs pages 85, 93) ○

by 🚗 only: up to 1h on foot. Park in Femés and follow Short walk 9 on page 85.

Picnic above the first crater (from where your views will be limited), or carry on to the summit another 25 minutes further up. From there you will have an excellent view of the volcanoes of Timanfaya and the south of the island — as well as the northern part of Fuerteventura. Note that this is a strenuous climb, and it can be very windy and cool!

10 DEGOLLADA DEL PORTUGUES (map pages 90-91, photograph page 96) ○

by 🚗 only: about 50min on foot. Park in Femés.
Follow Short walk 10 on page 89 to just over the 45min-point.
A very isolated setting overlooking the Barranco de los Dises, across to Hacha Grande.

11 PLAYA DE PAPAGAYO (map pages 90-91, photograph page 13) ○

by 🚗 only: 5min-1h on foot. From the roundabout by the Cepsa petrol station at Playa Blanca follow the gravel road east. Park near the hamlet above the beach (5min on foot). Since this road is very bumpy; you may prefer to park as suggested in Shorter walk 11 on page 96 (1h on foot).
Expect company here: Playa de Papagayo is mentioned in all the guides. There are good spots in the cove or on the rocky promontory to the right of the beach. Punta de Papagayo, less than 10 minutes beyond the hamlet, is always quiet, but usually windy. Playa de Puerto Muelas and the other beaches lining the coast also make splendid picnic spots.

12 MONTAÑA ROJA (map pages 104-105, photograph pages 100-101) ○

by 🚗 only: 40min on foot. Follow Walk 12, page 100.
Fine views over the Punta de Pechiguera and to Fuerteventura.

13 JANUBIO (map pages 104-105, photographs pages 103, 106) ○

by 🚌: 1h or more on foot. Bus to La Hoya; follow Walk 13, page 102.
by 🚗: 10-15min on foot. Park at the water desalination building off the CV road, some 2.4km south of the El Golfo roundabout.
Find a choice spot amidst the rocks fringing the shore. The beautiful rock pools lie about 10-15min southwest of the water desalination plant.

17 LOBOS (map page 121, photograph page 121) ○

by ⛴: 20min on foot. Boat from Playa Blanca to Lobos (see page 119).
Off the jetty, turn left. Less than 15min along you'll spot a path branching left into the dunes. This leads to lovely Playa de la Calera. If you prefer swimming from rocks, try the stunning setting of Casas El Puertito, just over 5min from the jetty (to the right). Both are superb, tranquil spots.

Cultivation at the foot of the path below the mirador at Haría (Picnic 5a) and (below) view from the Mirador del Río down over the salt pans and across to La Graciosa (Picnic 2 offers similar views).

 Touring

Hiring a vehicle is such good value on Lanzarote — and petrol so inexpensive — that it would be a pity not to take advantage of it. There are car rental offices in abundance in all the tourist centres.

Drive carefully! Excess speed is probably the main reason why *Lanzarote has the highest level of traffic accidents in all Spain.*

But as a tourist, your chief problem will be the poor signposting, especially on all the roundabouts built since the death of César Manrique. Manrique had argued for years that the Tahiche intersection on the main Arrecife/ Teguise road was dangerous, and that visitors to his foundation might be injured. In 1992 he was himself killed in a crash at this very spot. Since his death, roundabouts have been built all over the island. Unfortunately, while many of them are, literally, works of art, some are extremely complicated (especially for the newly-arrived visitor) and poorly signposted. *Remember, too:* traffic already on the roundabout has priority.

Another hazard is the deep unprotected drop at the side of some newly-surfaced roads, which is not always obvious when you screech to a halt and pull over at an 'unofficial' view-point, but you risk losing your transmission!

The touring notes are brief: they contain little history or information readily available in free tourist

Isolated farm near Timanfaya

office leaflets or standard guides. The main tourist centres and towns are not described either, for the same reason. Instead, I concentrate on the 'logistics' of touring: times and distances, road conditions, and seeing places many tourists miss. Most of all I emphasise possibilities for **walking** and **picnicking**. While some of the references to picnics off the beaten track may not be suitable during a long car tour, you may see a landscape that you would like to explore at leisure another day, when you've more time to stretch your legs.

The large fold-out touring map is designed to be held out opposite the touring notes and contains all the information you will need outside the towns. The tours have been written up starting from Puerto del Carmen, but I also suggest where best to join them if you are based as Playa Blanca or Costa Teguise. Town plans with exits for motorists are on pages 6-9. Remember to allow plenty of time for visits, and to take along warm clothing as well as some food and drink, in case you are delayed. The distances quoted in the notes are cumulative from Puerto del Carmen. A key to **symbols** used in the touring notes is on the touring map.

All motorists should read the country code on page 18 and go quietly in the countryside. *Buen viaje!*

A country code for walkers and motorists

The experienced rambler is used to following a 'country code', but the tourist out for a lark may unwittingly cause damage, harm animals, and even endanger his own life. Please heed this advice.

- **Do not light fires.**
- **Do not frighten animals.** The goats and sheep you may encounter on your walks are not tame.
- **Walk quietly** through all hamlets and villages.
- **Leave all gates just as you find them.** Although you may not see any animals, the gates do have a purpose — generally to keep goats or sheep in (or out of) an area.
- **Protect all wild and cultivated plants.** Don't try to pick wild flowers or uproot saplings. Obviously fruit and other crops are someone's private property and should not be touched. Never walk over cultivated land.
- **Take all your litter away with you.**
- **Walkers — *Do not take risks!*** This is the most important point of all. Do not attempt walks beyond your capacity, and do not wander off the paths described here if there is any sign of mist or if it is late in the day. Do *not* walk alone, and *always* tell a responsible person exactly where you are going and what time you plan to return. Remember, if you become lost or injure yourself, it may be a long time before you are found. On any but a very short walk close to villages, be sure to take a whistle, torch, extra water and warm clothing — as well as some high-energy food, like chocolate. Read and re-read the important note on page 2, as well as the guidelines on grade and equipment for each walk you plan to do!

Haría's Valle de los Castillejos (Picnic 5b), with Máguez and Monte Corona in the background

1 THE SIGHTS OF THE NORTH

Puerto del Carmen • Tahiche • Arrieta • Jameos del Agua • Cueva de los Verdes • Orzola • Mirador del Río • Haría • Teguise • La Caleta de Famara • Mozaga • Puerto del Carmen

143km/89mi; about 3h30min driving; Exit A from Puerto del Carmen

On route: roadside picnics at a chapel near Orzola, in Haría, or at El Bosquecillo; also Picnics 2, 3, 4, 5a, 5b, 6a, 6b (see pages 10-14 and **P** symbol in the text); Walks 2-6, 14

Although the driving time is only three and one-half hours, allow an entire day for this tour if you want to visit all the tourist attractions. Roads are generally good, but often narrow. Cloud and mist are not infrequent in the northern hills, and visibility can be reduced to almost zero! Look out for livestock on the roads and for pedestrians in the villages. A low speed is recommended for these roads. Arrecife is not included in this tour because it is well served by public transport and may be visited another day.

From Costa Teguise take the Guatiza road (LZ34) and join the tour on the LZ1 after passing through the arch with the cross. **From Playa Blanca** take the LZ2 and join the tour as you pass above the airport.

Opening hours

Cactus Garden, Guatiza: 10-18.00 daily
Jameos del Agua: 11.00-18.45 daily
Cueva de los Verdes: 10-17.00 daily
Mirador del Río (bar): 10.00-17.45 daily
Museo de Arte Sacro de Haría: 11.00-13.00 daily
Guinate Tropical Park: 10.00-17.00 daily
Castillo de Santa Bárbara, Teguise (Museo del Emigrante Canario): 10.00-16.00 (Tue-Fri); 11.00-15.00 (Sat/Sun); closed Mondays
Palacio Spinola, Teguise: 09.00-15.00 (Mon, Tues, Thur, Fri); 09.30-13.30 (Sat/Sun); closed Wednesdays
Villa Agrícola, Tiagua: 10.00-17.00 (Mon-Fri); 10.00-14.30 (Sat)

Apart from the Timanfaya National Park and the Geria Valley, the northern part of Lanzarote is the most scenically interesting. As you follow this tour, winding your way around and over the northern massif, you'll encounter the extraordinarily beautiful colours, shapes and textures that create the landscape canvas of Lanzarote. The Cueva de los Verdes — a vast volcanic tube measuring one kilometre in length, may be the most intriguing cave you've ever seen. You'll also learn who César Manrique was and what he meant to the island — or, rather, what his native land meant to him.

We leave Puerto del Carmen by heading east on the Avenida de las Playas (Exit A). Follow 'Arrecife'. As you pass a sign denoting the end of Puerto del Carmen, Canary date palms line both sides of the road and you are heading towards Montaña Blanca on the left and Montaña Mina on the right — with the wind generators that were a 'pilot project' for the larger installation we'll see later in the tour. As you approach a roundabout/flyover, keep right for Arrecife. This takes you onto the LZ2 (7km), and you drive above the airport. Watch for the km2 stone and get into the left-hand lane for 'circunvalación' *before* the Cepsa petrol stations. You join the LZ3 and see Mobil petrol stations on both sides of the road almost at once. Now ignore a sign right for Arrecife; keep ahead for 'San Bartolomé'. Ignore the LZ20 right for La Santa. Go under a footbridge and then a road. Just beyond this, keep straight on for 'Tahiche', ignoring a right turn for Arrecife. *But just past this turn for Arrecife, fork right for Orzola* (**easily missed**). After 2km you come upon the 'whirling whisks' roundabout shown below left, where you go straight over for 'Tahiche'. (A left here leads to the Fundación Manrique, and it was at this junction that César Manrique was killed in 1992.)

Just inside **Tahiche** (20km ✕) turn right for 'Arrieta', joining the LZ1 and passing through an open flat countryside pierced by prominent isolated hills. Pass the road to Costa Teguise (Walk 14); from afar its gateway, with a cross on top, looks like a chapel. Approaching the Moorish-flavoured village of **Guatiza** (29km) we come into cultivated fields and gardens squared off by stone walls. The village itself is swallowed up amidst fields of prickly pear. Leaving the village, pass the cactus garden (**Jardín de Cactus★**) on your right; a well-preserved windmill stands above it. Soon the entire plain is taken over by prickly pear. Farmed pricky pear is an unusual sight — normally we see it growing wild. The cochineal insect

Some roundabouts are such works of art that one can forgive them for being confusing! These 'wind sculptures' are both by César Manrique (left: just south of Tahiche; right: Arrieta). See also page 4.

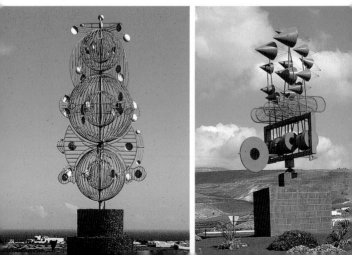

The Parque Eólico on the LZ10 is beautifully landscaped

is bred on these plants: the female lives off the juice of the cactus leaf (see photograph page 71), and after three months is harvested and dried in the sun. Today cochineal is used as colouring in lipsticks, toothpastes, and some drinks — Campari, for instance. The dye was once important in the carpet industry and during the 1800s was a major money-earner for Lanzarote. Off the sea-plain you look up into ridges that trail off the northern hills. **Mala** (32km ✗; Walk 6), another spacious farming village, follows. The 'Lanzarote colours' can be seen in the white façades and green doorways and window shutters of the houses. After leaving the village you pass a road up left to Tabayesco.*

In need of eggs, saucepans, or perhaps a fax machine? Then just pull into the petrol station in **Arrieta** (37km 🚇✗▲), a small seaside village built along the rocky shore. At the roundabout just past here, the revolving red cones shown opposite are another of Manrique's confections. Follow 'Orzola', then bear right almost immediately for Jameos del Agua, ignoring the road left to the Mirador del Río. Pass **Punta Mujeres** (38km ✗), a tight cluster of dwellings with more than its fair share of restaurants. A few minutes later we branch off right for **Jameos del Agua★** (42km ✗), one of the island's most frequented tourist attractions. This enchanting cave is the result of two opposing forces — man and nature. A splendid compromise has been reached: the eruption of Monte Corona was responsible for the natural element; César Manrique was the man. The cave has been skillfully transformed into a night club, maintaining as much natural décor as possible. Penetrating into the depths of the cave, you come to a large crystal-clear sea-pool. Shiny objects on the floor of the pool catch your eye: tiny white blind crabs *(Munidopsis poliforma)*, unique in the sea world.

*Sometime during your visit, make a circuit of the beautiful Chafariz Valley (photograph page 24): turn up this road (📻) and, when you come into Haría, turn right for 'Arrieta'. Descending the far side of the valley, you rejoin the main road by the 'red cones' roundabout shown opposite.

Jameos del Agua

You then ascend to this swimming pool, set in a colourful rock garden.

Return to the main road, cross it, and head up to the **Cueva de los Verdes★**, 1km away. Only one of the seven kilometres of this vast complex of tunnels is open to the public. With a guide, you wind down through low, narrow passageways and emerge into enormous cool chambers — one of them an auditorium with perfect acoustics. The Guanches sought refuge in these caves whenever there were pirate raids. The caves were created when streams of molten lava flowed beneath a hardened outside crust (see pages 113-115).

Back on the main road, turn left for Orzola. Following the coast, we run along the edge of the Malpais ('Badlands') de la Corona — an expansive undulating plateau of lava carpeted in a thick mat of greenery. Monte Corona — a massive sharp-rimmed crater that dominates the north of the island — broods lonely and impressive on the left. Patches of sand and a couple of sandy coves embraced in the rocky shoreline break up the lava flow (photograph pages 116-117). Soon the table-topped island of Alegranza appears over to your right — and the north of La Graciosa. Rocky reefs create lagoons along the shoreline, and these are ideal for swimming.

The Famara massif rises up into a bold block of hills behind **Orzola** (53km ▲✕ and ⛴ to La Graciosa) and its port. Here's where you catch the ferry, if you're planning to do Walk 1 or picnic on La Graciosa. There's also a pleasant coastal walk to Punta Fariones; see page 116.

Now making for the Mirador del Río, we climb inland, after 500m passing a chapel on the left, a pleasant picnic spot with some shade. Still circling the *malpais* on a narrow winding road, a wavy blanket of greenery, pierced by rocky outcrops, stretches below. We rejoin the LZ1 at the foot of Monte Corona and ascend to the right. Thick stone walls soon take over the countryside; their precision transforms the fields into a work of art. An imposing solitary villa, the Torrecilla del Domingo, rises up out of this maze of walls, crowning a hilltop. We pass above the Quemada crater; Walk 3 circles it. On the outskirts of Ye, a small farming community cast across a sloping plateau below Corona's gaping crater, turn right again for 'Mirador del Río'. Crossing the plateau, you look straight down into deep valleys. In spring the top of the plateau is flecked with poppies, daisies and *Echium*.

A porthole window set in a stone wall enclosing the car park is all that gives away the **Mirador del Río★** (📷; paid admission), built on the site of a 16th-century watchtower. This well-camouflaged viewpoint is embedded in the top of the **Risco** (Cliff) **de Famara★**. From here you look straight out over the Río channel onto the bare and barren — yet strangely beautiful — Graciosa Island, which sits just below (photographs pages 50 and 55). This is a view unequalled on Lanzarote, and one of the best vistas in all the Canaries. The mountain island (Montaña Clara) and Alegranza enhance this already-magnificent sea view. The *mirador* balcony hangs out over a precipitous wall plummeting 450m/1475ft below … down to the landscapes of Walk 2 — the exquisite Playa del Risco and the captivating salt pans of El Río. Note: the exterior of this setting is worth seeing from the cliff-top above the *mirador* (from where the photographs below and on page 15 were taken).

You must pay to visit the Mirador del Río. At time of writing, it was possible to walk to the left of the mirador and climb over a wall to see this 'view of views', but it is likely that this path will be closed in future. Note also that many maps show a footpath north of the mirador to a trig point above Punta Fariones, but this route is barred, and there are guards around to make sure you don't try to climb over the wall.

From the *mirador* fork right, to continue south along the edge of the Famara cliffs. This wall of rock stretches for 23km and reaches a height of 600m/1970ft, as it slices its way along the northwest coast. The road is narrow, but built up at the sides; priority is given to traffic travelling in this direction. You recapture the very dramatic *mirador* vista a little further on, where you are able to pull over safely. In the distance ahead you see the vast Jable plain stretching inland behind the Playa de Famara, and the hills growing up out of the west coast.

Leaving the plateau we overlook a rocky basin of farmland on the far side of Ye. Some 2.4km from the *mirador* we pass the stone-laid track to the most stunning picnic spot on the island (***P***2) — also set in these cliffs. After another 200m, just below Monte Corona, come to a stop sign at a T-junction and turn right for Haría. Pass the turn-off to the Guinate Tropical Park, where the circuit of Los Helechos (***P***4 and Walk 4) ends — by car or on foot. When you come to a Y-fork, keep right for 'Arrecife' (but to park for ***P***3, in the setting shown on page 60, go left.)

Máguez (72km ✗; photographs page 62-63) is a rambling, pleasantly scruffy country village with a peaceful air about it. Walk 4 circles the very quiet and scenic mound of volcanoes up to the right. Keep straight on through the village, and take care at the stop sign in the centre, where buildings totally obscure your view of crossing traffic.

Over in the next valley lies **Haría** (74km ✗**M*P***5b), the handsome settlement shown on pages 1, 15, 18, and 68-69. This oasis of greenery boasts the largest number of palms in the Canaries. (I wonder what La Gomera has to

Barranco de Chafariz (see footnote page 21)

César Manrique's simple grave at the cemetery in Haría (left) and the Ermita de las Nieves

say about this?) Bougainvillea, geraniums, and hibiscus splash the village with colour, and the grand shady plaza adds a touch of class. Keep right on coming into the village and at the T-junction in front of the town hall, turn right, then immediately left, for 'Teguise'. Just as you leave the village, you could picnic opposite the grounds of the Villa Dolores (ample parking, a wall to sit on, shade). Exiting this valley of palms we wind up a rocky crest in tight hairpins. Some 4km uphill you will spot a white building ahead with the inscription 'Mirador de Haría', but there's hardly room to park. Don't worry: continue for 1km more, to the superb viewpoint at the Restaurante los Helechos (79km 🖼✕**P**5a), where Walk 5 starts. Some 200m past the restaurant, ignore a rough road off to the right signposted 'Ermita de las Nieves' (it is climbed in Alternative walk 5-2). Soon we head below Lanzarote's highest point, the Peñas del Chache (670m/2200ft), which houses a miltary installation. Save for the 'golf balls' on top, you'd hardly notice it. What *does* catch the eye are the wind generators of the Parque Eólico ahead.

Just under 3km from the Helechos *mirador*, turn right on a good road signposted 'Ermita de las Nieves'. This 18th-century chapel (**P**6a; photographs above and page 12) stands in solitude, high on a windswept plateau, marking the site where the Virgin appeared to a young shepherd. The chapel is open on Saturdays between 14.30 and 18.00 and on the patron saint's day in September. From the edge of the plateau you have a splendid view down onto the extensive Playa de Famara and over the semi-desert Jable plain. The Risco de Famara topples off to an abrupt end here.*

Head back to the main road, passing the charmingly-landscaped gardens of the Parque Eólico. Stone walls fence off the countryside on our approach to Los Valles. The interior of the island opens up, as low-slung valleys peel back and rounded hillocks rise in the background. Serried ranks of American aloes line the road as it descends in curves (✕). **Los Valles** (88km) sits on the edge of a sweeping basin patched in huge cultivated squares. Here we find the best examples of the traditional Arcadian houses — low oblong buildings with very few (and very small) windows. Cocks (haystacks) set amidst the houses and farm buildings set off this rural landscape.

Beyond Los Valles we cross the basin as we head towards Teguise. Rising ahead on the left is the 16th-century Castillo de Santa Bárbara (🏰). This modest fortress commands a good view over the surrounding countryside from its perch at the edge of the Guanapay crater. Once a watchtower to warn against the raiding Moors, it now houses a small museum dedicated to the Canarian emigrant. Below, to the right, you will see some substantial honey-hued ruins — the old Ermita de San José (**P**6b).

Walk 6 ends at **Teguise★** (95km ✕♣M), the island's ancient capital … and Lanzarote's showplace. The village still retains its original character of cobbled streets, stately old buildings, and spacious plazas. In the main square you'll find the imposing Church of San Miguel, facing the 18th-century Palacio Spinola. The convents of Santo Domingo and San Francisco are in amongst the houses.

Leaving the glaring whiteness of Teguise, bear right for Mozaga, to get on the LZ30 (🚍). Some 3km out of town, turn right for 'La Caleta'. Now we make for the coast. The dusty fishing village of **La Caleta de Famara** (112km ⚓✕) boasts some fine seafood restaurants. (To reach the quieter end of this long black-sand beach, drive through the *urbanización* and follow the track below the cliffs. Alternative walk 2 ends here.)

From La Caleta make for Tiagua on the LZ401. Beyond **Sóo** and **Munique** you pass the Villa Agrícola, a museum

---

*Another splendid picnic spot, El Bosquecillo ('the Little Wood'; 📷🏕), lies nearby, off a rough track. To get there, take the motorable track behind the chapel, pass the military area, and then fork left on a rougher track for 'Mirador'. Keep right at all other forks. This shaded viewpoint, with a few tables, is perched at the top of the Famara cliffs and is very popular with the locals on weekends.)

of countryside life, before coming into **Tiagua** (✕). Turn left on the LZ20 towards 'Arrecife'. At **Mozaga** (✕ 🚘) you come to a roundabout at the Monumento al Campesino★ (see Tour 2) and go straight over to **San Bartolomé**. From here keep straight through on the LZ20 to the Arrecife ring road, then retrace your outgoing route, coming back into **Puerto del Carmen** after 143km.

Church at Teguise; see also photograph pages 74-75.

2 TIMANFAYA AND THE SOUTHERN BEACHES

Puerto del Carmen • San Bartolomé • Tinajo • La Santa • Montañas del Fuego • Yaiza • El Golfo • Playa Blanca • Papagayo • Femés • La Geria Valley • San Bartolomé • Puerto del Carmen

150km/93mi; 4 hours driving (plus 1 hour's coach tour in the national park); Exit B from Puerto del Carmen

On route: roadside picnics at La Isleta, El Golfo, Femés, La Geria; also Picnics 8-13 (see pages 10-14 and *P* symbol in the text); Walks 7-13, 15

Roads are good with two exceptions: the road in the Geria valley is narrow and drops off sharply at the sides, into the vineyards below. Take special care here: the scenery is so eye-catching that you could easily drive off the road. The rough track to Papagayo (a minimum of 6km each way) is only recommended for beach enthusiasts; it's very bumpy and also on the route of jeep safaris — you'll taste a lot of dust when they pass. Between Yaiza and Playa Blanca this tour follows the old road (CV); the newer LZ2 is the 'fast track'.

From Costa Teguise take the Arrecife ring road and join the tour at San Bartolomé (the 11km-point). From Playa Blanca begin at the round-about by the Cepsa petrol station: take the 'old road' (CV) signposted to Yaiza and, at the junction for El Golfo, turn off for Las Breñas, joining the tour on page 35 and finishing the circuit when you return to Playa Blanca.

Opening hours
Timanfaya National Park: 09.00-17.00 daily, with coach tours from 09.00-16.00 daily, every half hour (included in the entry fee)
Timanfaya Visitors' Centre, Mancha Blanca: 09.00-17.00 daily
Monumento al Campesino (house and museum): 10.00-18.00 daily; restaurant 12-17.00 daily
Museo del Vino (Masdache): 10.00-18.00 daily

This southern route allows you plenty of time for short strolls, a swim, and perhaps some wine-tasting — if you make a day of it. Vulcanology may not be one of your favourite topics, but this drive will certainly arouse your interest in it. Violent eruptions in the 18th and 19th centuries have left a curious landscape in their wake. The national park bus tour — a must for everyone — immerses you in this moonscape of rich volcanic hues. It will be the highlight of your day, if not of your entire holiday on Lanzarote. More

Vineyards in La Geria lead the eye to the Fire Mountains of Timanfaya

28

curiosities follow, however. La Geria, the valley of ash, and the home of *malvasía* wine, is another amazing sight. Here the vineyards create a scenery of their own. The eroded Golfo crater, with its dazzling green lagoon, is something akin to an artist's palette, with all its colours and blended hues. And if all this isn't enough, then there are the golden sandy beaches of the southeast, of which Papagayo has become the most popular amongst tourists. You'll soon see why.

Leave Puerto del Carmen on the Tías road (Exit B). Follow signs for Tías at first, then San Bartolomé — through a nightmare of poorly-signposted roundabouts. We bypass Tías and wind up over hills into a vast sloping valley, with Montaña Blanca to the left and Montaña Mina ahead to the right, crowned with wind generators. Vivid splashes of scarlet poppies, white daisies, and yellow dandelions light up the surrounding farmlands. Head straight through the sprawling village of **San Bartolomé** (11km ✕), keeping to the right of the main square and, when you meet the LZ20, turn left for Tinajo.

At a roundabout (14km ✕🚭) we're confronted with another of Manrique's works — the Monumento al Campesino★, dedicated to the island's country dwellers. This bold structure (photograph page 4) stands in pleasant surroundings, with a restaurant (a beautifully-restored farmhouse) that specialises in local dishes, a souvenir

shop, and a small 'farmyard' of great appeal to children. On the far side of the roundabout, we come into the hamlet of **Mozaga**. The setting is very picturesque: the houses are dispersed amidst great blocks of lava, which are brightly speckled with green *Aeoniums*. Neat, fresh-green garden plots border the lava plain.

Tao (17km ✗ 📷) occupies a slight rise with a fine view across the sweeping Jable plain to the cliffs of Famara and the islands. A sprinkling of elegant palms complements this pleasant rural setting. We pass through **Tiagua** (18km ✗M) in the thick of these gardens.

An avenue of Canary date palms leads us into the expansive farming settlement of **Tinajo** (23km ✗🚌), where Walk 7 ends. Entering the village, turn right for La Santa at the roundabout. Descending to the coast, the red Montaña Bermeja catches your eye, rising off the shore below to the left. The countryside becomes harsher, rough and bumpy with hillocks, and the terrain is strewn with stones. **La Santa** (✗) is a small village of restaurants set back off the shore. Continue to Club La Santa, a rather exclusive sports complex 2km further on (30km ⛰✗). It overlooks the rocky islet, La Isleta, and a pretty lagoon — a pleasant interlude in this desolate stretch of coast. To cross to the *isleta,* curve left past the hotel reception and when you come to a roundabout, keep right. Circle halfway round the islet; then, keeping the lagoon just to your left, return to the main road. Opposite is a large parking area under palms; you can picnic here on lava jetties near the sea or by the lagoon.

Returning to Tinajo, keep straight on through the village for 'Mancha Blanca', soon enjoying a pretty view left to the small village of La Vegueta. Just as you enter **Mancha Blanca** (41km; starting point for Walk 7), turn right for 'Yaiza, Montañas del Fuego'. Mancha Blanca rests on a shelf overlooking its tidy ash fields, on the edge of a sea of lava that floods the southwest. Everything here grows in straight rows, as you can see in the photograph on page 76-77. The village is the home of the island's female patron saint — Our Lady of the Volcanoes, who is credited with having saved Tinajo from a lava flow. A popular festival celebrates the saint's day on September 15th each year.

At 43.5km we enter the national park; the Visitors' Centre is 100m along on the right. Even if you're not going to book for Walk 15, *do* stop here to see the audio-visual show and study the exhibits, to better appreciate the land-

On the coach trip through the Ruta de los Volcanes, you will be able to get off and take photographs.

scape which lies ahead! Beyond the Visitors' Centre we mount the lava plateau, where another world awaits us: the world of fire and brimstone, where over 250 years ago all hell let loose and (as Yaiza's parish priest described it) 'the earth suddenly opened up and an enormous mountain rose from the bosom of the earth and from its apex shot flames which continued to burn for 19 days'. This catastrophic eruption lasted intermittently for some six years (1730 to 1736), burying one-third of the island (including eleven villages) under metres of lava … an eruption unsurpassed in recorded history. Less than one hundred years later another eruption increased the existing number of volcanoes from 26 to 29.

Crossing this lonely but curiously beautiful landscape (photographs pages 16-17 and 110-115) is like being on another planet, hence it should come as no surprise to learn that the first astronauts were shown photographs of the national park in preparation for their moon flight. The road cuts its way through rough, sharp 'AA' lava. Lichen flecks the rock, creating the impression of freshly fallen sleet. Pale pink wild geraniums stand out poignantly in this black world. Their leaves are dried by the locals and made into tea — a good source of vitamin C. Assorted volcanoes, with hints of red, clay brown, and deep maroon, grow out of the lava.

Large mounds of cinder soon close in on us. Some 9km from Mancha Blanca, at a mini-roundabout, we turn off right for the **Islote de Hilario** — departure point for the coach tours around the **Montañas del Fuego★**. An entrance fee, which includes the tour, is paid here. The *islote*

is named for the hermit Hilario, who returned here after the eruptions had subsided to build a hut and plant a fig tree (which, incidentally, is *not* the fig in the restaurant). The restaurant here makes good use of thermal energy — the temperature reaches 360°C only six metres below the surface of the ground. Your excursion bus twists up, down, and around the great volcanoes, affording stunning views over the park and into the craters, which drip with endless blends of colours.

Leaving the Islote de Hilario and continuing south, we pass alongside the russet-brown slopes of Pico Timanfaya (also called Pico del Fuego). Both the mountain and the park take their name from the village of Timanfaya, which thrived in this rich agricultural area before being destroyed by the eruptions. After 2km we pass the starting point for the much-publicised camel rides. You're bound to see a camel train ascending or descending — complete with awkwardly-seated tourists. It's an impressive sight, no matter how 'touristic'. Also, notice the lava formation on the left-hand side of the road here, with great cracks in its crust: this is *pahoehoe* lava (the name is Hawaiian).

Out of the lava fields come to a roundabout and cross the LZ2, to enter the charming white-washed village of **Yaiza** (61km ✗🛒⊕♿). Beyond the petrol station, turn right at the junction. You pass the cool, shady Los Remedios Square, with an 18th-century church of the same name. This proud village (see also photograph pages 86-87) has some fine old balconied houses, and the gardens overflow with colour. Walk 9 begins and ends here. On the outskirts of the village take the El Golfo exit from the roundabout. We enter more jagged lava fields; these are interrupted by *islotes* (islands of lava-free ground).

Meet the road to El Golfo and bear right. Bushes of resplendent green *tabaiba* light up the encompassing dark lava. Crossing a crest, an unmarked *mirador* just before the village gives you an excellent view over the eroded

Golfo craters. This majestic submarine volcano has been spectacularly eaten away by the sea, leaving one with the impression that it has been sliced in half. **El Golfo★** (69km ✕📷) is a cheerful seaside village of restaurants — the ideal place to finish the Timanfaya coastal walk from Playa de la Madera described on page 118. Return to the junction for the village and head right for 'Playa Blanca'. At a T-junction some 2km along, turn right (signposted 'Charco de los Clicos') to the parking area for the *golfo,* a crescent-shaped bay. Strolling down to the crater, you're greeted by a striking sight: an array of greys, browns, and reds oozes out of the cone and surrounding rock. A strong blue sea and a cloudy green lagoon (the Charco de los Clicos)★ set at the base of the crater enhance this rainbow of colours (photographs pages 10-11 and overleaf). Although the area is fairly crowded, few people stay very long, and there are many pleasant picnic perches, with shade from the cliffs.

Following the coastline further south, we drive through billowing waves of lava. The colourful Montaña Bermeja soon commands your attention with its glowing orange-brown cone. Just over 2km from El Golfo's crater, turn right to a large parking area for **Los Hervideros★** (📷; the 'boiling springs'), where the sea pounds into sea-caves. Walkways have been carefully laid out through the maze of lava, where there are some impressive blow-holes when the sea is choppy. The sight is all the more impressive with the bright cone of Montaña Bermeja in the background. The lazy hills of Los Ajaches, leaning one against the other, rise up prominently ahead. Las Breñas is the village you see sprinkled along a raised shelf at the foot of the hills.

Turning inland, we round the **Salinas de Janubio★** (📷). They lie cradled in a deep basin off a land-locked lagoon and the curving black sand beach of Janubio. You look down onto a fine mosaic of tiny white squares of drying salt and ponds. The colours of this basin turn the severe countryside into quite a beauty spot, especially in the evening (see photograph page 106). Beyond the third viewpoint over the pans, you come to a roundabout at **La Hoya**: go right for 'Playa Blanca' on the CV. Some 600m along, a crest jutting out above the lagoon (a signposted *mirador;* 📷) enables you to view the *salinas* from the other side. This is the setting for Walk 13. Then, 1.8km from the *mirador,* you pass an isolated water desalination building (**P**13), from where you can also reach Walk 13.

Now crossing the featureless, stone-strewn Rubicón plain, we reach **Playa Blanca** (98km 🏔🏔🛏✕🍴 and 🚢 to Fuerteventura), once a small fishing village, but now swallowed up by a mass of bungalows, hotels, apartments … and the sad remains of urbanizations that were never built. Fuerteventura sits enticingly close — just a 40-minute ferry trip away.

The track to Papagayo is signposted on the east side

of the roundabout with the Cepsa petrol station just outside Playa Blanca. *Be warned:* this bumpy track is a jeep safari route. You might prefer to walk to Papagayo (see Shorter walk 11) — or even to take a cruise there another day (boats leave from the port at Playa Blanca). If you *do*

Charco de los Clicos and the El Golfo crater — a fascinating example of marine erosion. See also pages 10-11.

decide to drive there, ignore tracks branching off in all directions to various beaches. Stay on the main track, just by following everyone else. You'll cross a barren stony shelf that lies at the foot of the Ajaches. All the beaches along here are different, and all are enticing. Before reaching Papagayo, branch off left to Playa de Puerto Muelas (better known to tourists as 'La Caleta'). This is the unofficial — and, needless to say, very popular — naturist beach. **Papagayo**, with its few derelict houses, is the hippy hangout. All the other beaches are for you and me (*P*11; photograph page 13).

Femés, our next destination, *can* be reached via a dusty gravel road that cuts across the Rubicón from Papagayo. But I don't recommend this further bone-splintering ride unless you have a jeep. It's more comfortable to go via Las Breñas. So we return to the El Golfo roundabout and turn right, immediately going under the LZ2. On entering **Las Breñas**, keep left at the first fork, to pass the pretty church. Coming back down to the main road at a T-junction, turn left. Soon the road climbs straight towards an antenna-topped hill, the Atalaya de Femés (*P*9). A superb panorama over the plain to Playa Blanca and out to Fuerteventura unfolds. You see the 'pimply' island of Lobos and the white dunes of Corralejo directly behind it. The hills tower above you, with ridges tumbling out of them in all directions. The road zigzags up to a narrow pass, and just on the saddle sits **Femés** (118km ✕ ⌕), overlooking the flat Rubicón plain. Your view is framed by the encircling hills. Take a break and enjoy the vista from this *mira-dor*. The church is dedicated to San Marcial, the island's patron saint, and the lovely church square is an ideal spot for a picnic if you don't want to huff and puff your way up the Atalaya! Femés is a precious little village, set high up in an already elevated valley

Los Hervideros, with the colourful cone of Montaña Bermeja in the background.

and shut off from the rest of the island. Walks 9, 10 and 11 converge on Femés (see photographs pages 85-95).

Continuing through fields, we drop down out of the valley and onto the LZ2. Cross straight over the main road and then continue straight ahead at the junction, on the narrower LZ30 (for *P*8 park 50m past the km22 stone). **Uga** (124km ✗), down to the left, is a colourful village with a North African flavour about it. It rests in a saucer of gardens with its back up against the dark lava sea of the Timanfaya National Park. Rounding a corner, the scenery changes yet again, as we enter the intriguing valley of **La Geria★**, a dark sweeping depression, further pitted with hollows. The slopes are coated in black ash. Myriad low half-moon stone walls edge the hollows and stretch across the countryside (see also photograph on pages 80-81). This is the home of *malvasía* wine, the product of an ingenious farming method: the vines are planted in crater-like depressions layered with *lapilli,* which absorb the moisture from the air and enable a single vine to produce up to as much as 200 kilos of grapes annually. *(Note: concentrate on the road; pull over when you want to 'ooh' and 'aah'.)* There are several *bodegas* along this road. If you're longing for a shady spot to picnic, watch out, just past Bodegas António Suarez and the km18 stone, for a eucalpytus-shaded ruin on the right. At 130.5km ignore the right turn to Macher and, shortly after, a left turn to Mancha Blanca.*

Leaving La Geria, we re-enter the lava — this time 'ropey' *pahoehoe* lava, characterised by surface ripples created when molten lava flowed beneath the solidified outer crust (see page 114). Strips of encroaching 'AA' lava, encrusted with lichen, give the effect of stagnant, weed-infested ponds. Cheerful green *Aeoniums* freckle the landscape. **Masdache** (135km ✗) lies amidst this upheaval of lava. Here's your chance to do some wine-tasting, at the Wine Museum on the outskirts of the village. But remember: you still have to drive home! A row of prominent, gaping craters lines the landscape on your right. Re-entering vineyards and vegetable gardens, serenity returns to the countryside. A couple of kilometres beyond Masdache, at a pretty, palm-filled junction, we bear right for **San Bartolomé**, where we rejoin this morning's route and return to **Puerto del Carmen** (150km).

*The road left to Mancha Blanca is worth exploring another day, as is the road from El Grifo which runs north to La Vegueta. Both are very scenic, with fine examples of *pahoehoe* lava (see photograph page 114.)

3 A DAY OUT ON FUERTEVENTURA

Playa Blanca • Corralejo • Dunes Natural Park • (Puerto del Rosario) • Castillo de Fustes • La Antigua • Tuineje • Pájara • Puerto de la Peña • Betancuria • La Oliva • (El Cotillo) • Lajares • Corralejo • Playa Blanca

190km/118mi; 6 hours driving (plus 50min each way on the ferry and any driving on Lanzarote to reach Playa Blanca)

On route: Picnic by the Presa de las Peñitas, or have lunch at Pájara — a popular coach stop, but where you can avoid the crowds.

*This is a **very** long day. **Do** plan on taking the first ferry in the morning and returning on the last one. There is no need to pre-book; just turn up about half an hour before sailing time and buy your tickets at the office on the pier at Playa Blanca. Either fill up with petrol at the roundabout just outside Playa Blanca, or in Corralejo. This tour takes in the sights of the north and middle of Fuerteventura — it's just not practicable to get to the Jandía Peninsula as well on a day trip from Lanzarote. To visit Jandía, you should spend at least one night on the island. Puerto del Rosario, the capital, is only included as an optional detour — I concentrate on the **countryside**. Roads are all good, but the road between Pájara and the Vega de Río Palmas is narrow, with very sheer drops, and not always protected at the side; some motorists might find it unnerving. See map of northern Fuerteventura and plan of Corralejo on the reverse of the Lanzarote touring map inside the back cover.*

Get up with the birds to make the most of this day — not only to get value from the cost of your ferry crossing, but to take in the best landscapes. After spending a week or so on Lanzarote, Fuerteventura comes as a bit of a shock! Lanzarote's landscapes are so neatly-manicured, so bright-white, so *tidy*. Corralejo, by contrast, looks ramshackle and dusty as you bump your way off the ferry. And Fuerteventura's landscapes are equally unkempt. You'll drive for miles and miles with hardly a sign of habitation — just rosey-red untamed hillsides, dotted with the odd palm or windmill. And when you *do* come

The Dunes Natural Park near Corralejo

upon settlements, you may be delighted to find a wealth of old buildings full of character and colour … even though some of them appear to be coming apart at the seams.

Leave Corralejo's port following signs for 'Puerto del Rosario' and 'Las Playas'. Joining the coastal road to Puerto del Rosario (FV1), you head out through the **Dunes Natural Park★**— white caster-sugar sands stretching as far as the eye can see. This stunning stretch of white shimmering sand is further enhanced by the aquamarine sea and the purply-blue hills that rise in the background. Lobos (Walk 17) stands out clearly on your left, offshore, with its hundreds of little hillocks and guardian volcano. The dunes are supposedly a natural park, but all the same, two hotels interrupt this unique stretch of beauty (▲▲✕).

Out of this mini-desert, we cross a featureless stone-littered plain. At 19km pass a turn-off to Parque Holandés (▲✕): a number of tourist booklets recommend a visit, but I would advise you to skip it. This tour also bypasses Puerto del Rosario (▲▲▲✕✝🚰⊕); it has little to offer, being visibly the poorest town on the island. So on your approach to the capital, keep following 'aeropuerto', to stay on the ring road, the FV3. Watch for your turn-off: filter right for 'aeropuerto' and 'Morro del Jable' (37.5km): this takes you back to the coastal road (FV2 🚰) and you pass the *parador* on the left at 39km (▲▲).

Caleta de Fustes/El Castillo (▲▲▲✕⊕) is a popular tourist centre. To see the best (older) part of it, take the *second* turn-off, signposted 'Las Villas del Castillo'. A beautiful palm-lined road takes you to the circular 18th-century defense tower *(castillo)* by the little yachting harbour.

Continuing south on the main road, at 65km turn right for La Antigua on the FV50. On coming to a main road (🚰) turn right again, into **La Antigua** (74km ✝✕). The

38

Two sights not to be missed: the Colonels' house at La Oliva (left) and the door of Pájara's church

square is beautifully laid out; the church simple but imposing nevertheless. Just north of La Antigua (on the FV20, the Puerto del Rosario road) stands El Molino★ (✖), a well-preserved 200-year-old windmill, once used for grinding corn. The windmill is an appropriate introduction to La Antigua, because this area has the highest concentration of windmills on Fuerteventura — as you will see as you head south towards Tuineje on the FV20.

Out in the country again, palms return to the scene. A trickle of villages is seen sitting back in the plain. Threading our way through hills, we find cultivated fields sheltering along the floors of the *barrancos*. We pass some photogenic windmills (see page 44) on our route through **Valles de Ortega**, **Agua de Bueyes** and **Tiscamanita**. Three dark volcanoes, La Laguna, Liria and Los Arrabales, rupture the lake of lava that spills out over the plains on your left. This area is called the *malpaís* ('badlands'). Around **Tuineje** (86km 🚌) the large *fincas* of the tomato-growers are a prominent feature in a barren landscape.

Head out right on the FV30 towards Pájara. Rosy-rusty tones emanate from the landscape and are reflected in the honey-coloured stone of the walls and old ruins. We cross a col and a huge basin opens up ahead, with views to the sea. Down in the valley, on the approach to **Toto**, you'll spot 'wigwams' of palm fronds drying the in sun; the dry fronds are used for fencing and for basket-weaving.

Pájara (94km ✝✖ and swimming pool) is a large farming community surrounded by hills. The shady village is a welcoming sight, with its abundance of trees and small colourful gardens. Don't miss the church here; it is especially noteworthy for the striking 'Aztec' stone-carved decoration above the main entrance (see above). Quite a curiosity because, apart from similar sculptures in La Oliva, these carvings are unique in the Canary Islands. The two naves inside the church date back to 1645 and 1687, while the carving over the door is thought to date from the 1500s. Pájara is popular with the coach tour crowds, but Restaurante La Fonda, just opposite the church, is too small to seat them. If you haven't brought a picnic, it's a good place for lunch in quiet surroundings.

From Pájara take the FV621, to descend to Ajuy/Puerto de la Peña. Rounding a corner, we look down into a valley lush with palm trees, tamarisk shrubs and garden plots. Below **Ajuy** we come into **Puerto de la Peña** (103km), a small village set on the edge of a black sand beach. It's one of two fishing settlements on the west coast. Few tourists venture over to the dramatically-sited ancient port here. It hides in a bay some 15 minutes' walk around the coast to the south of the village.

From Puerto de la Peña return to Pájara, then take the road for Vega de Río de Palmas; it's at the left of the church. Again we ascend into the hills, climbing on a narrow winding road that hugs the sheer inclines (some people might find this road unnerving). There are excellent views back over the Barranco de Pájara. The Degollada de los Granadillos is the pass that takes us over a solid spur of rock that juts out into the valley below. From this pass you have a superb outlook over to the enclosing rocky ridges. Unfortunately, there is nowhere safe to park.

But soon, descending, we come to a large parking area overlooking the Presa de las Peñitas (📷), a muddy reservoir lodged in the V of the Barranco de las Peñitas. The reservoir looks deeper than it is; it's only about one metre (3ft) deep, as it has filled up with silt. Groves of tamarisk trees huddle around the tail of the presa, and that's a good spot from which to do some birdwatching. Green gardens step the sides of the slopes, and palm trees complement the scene. Below the reservoir lies a sheer-sided rocky ravine, the ideal hiding place for the chapel dedicated to the island's patron saint, Nuestra Señora de la Peña.

This impressive ravine is one of the island's beauty spots, so let's do more exploring. Past the

At the end of the road below the Vega de Río Palmas, a lovely picnic spot near the Presa de las Peñitas

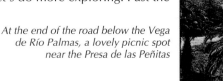

viewpoint, the rest of the valley opens up, and a string of *casas* stretches along it. They're set amidst a healthy sprinkling of palms and cultivated plots — a luxuriant corner. Turn down *sharp* left at the first road you come to, just before the centre of **Vega de Río de Palmas**. This 3km-long road is very narrow, but there is room for two cars to pass. When the tar runs out, continue on track to a turning area (before a chain bars the way). This is an exquisite picnic spot beside the reservoir, with shady palms and a symphony of birdsong.

Return to the main road, pass the church dedicated to Nuestra Señora de la Peña on the right, and continue twisting up the valley. The countryside subsides into rolling contours once again. Notice a large abandoned field of sisal on the hillsides on your left, a short distance further on. This crop was introduced from Mexico.

At the end of this valley we come to the village of **Betancuria★** (134km 🏕🏨✖M), well hidden from the marauding Berbers of earlier centuries. It's a very picturesque collection of manorial buildings, with a grand 17th-century cathedral. The cathedral and convent here are the oldest examples of their style in the archipelago. Relics abound in historic Betancuria, and I hope you'll notice some of them. A number of the old houses have doorways and arches dating back to the 15th century. Betancuria was the capital of Fuerteventura for some 400

years, up until 1835, and was also the first episcopal seat for all the Canaries. The oldest part of the village huddles around the cathedral — much of it slowly deteriorating. History-hunters will enjoy the cathedral and the small Museo Sacreo here — as well as the municipal museum.

Leaving Betancuria on the FV30, everyone passes by the Franciscan monastery, the shell of which sits below the road on the northern side of the village. Inside it (unseen from the road) are some beautiful cloistered arches. Near the convent is a small enclosed church — actually the first church on the island; however, much of the building was rebuilt in the 17th century.

We zigzag up out of the valley and pull over at the top of the pass (📷) for a fine panorama over a vast plain to the north. Its far-distant reaches are edged by sharp abrupt hills called *cuchillos* (knives); over on our left lie *morros* (low, smooth hills). Betancuria nestles cosily in the valley floor below.

Leaving the viewpoint, when you come to a round-about, turn left. Pass through **Valle de Santa Inés** and **Llanos de la Concepción**. At another roundabout go left for 'Tefia, La Oliva' (FV207). After passing between Montaña Bermeja on the left and Cuchillos on the right, mellow old stone walls and farmhouses introduce **Tefia**. Beyond the village, turn left on the FV10 for La Oliva. We next pass above **Tindaya** (✕). It spreads across a flattened crest amidst a profusion of faded brown stone walls. Behind the village stands captivating Montaña Tindaya, a great rocky salient that dominates the surrounding countryside with its boldness. Perhaps this is why the Guanches chose it as their holy mountain.

Left: on the approach to Betancuria.
Far left: Betancuria's 17th-century cathedral

At the other end of this plain lies the pleasant country village of **La Oliva**★ (166km ♣✕). It rests on the edge of a lava flow. Montaña Arena, a mountain of sand, rises up out of the lava in the background. Drive straight ahead to the church, where there's ample parking. Nuestra Señora de Candelaria overpowers the village with its solid black-stone belfry. La Oliva was a town of some importance in the 17th century, when the island's military post was stationed here. The official residence (the Colonels' House) can be seen abandoned on the outskirts of the village (follow signs for the art centre). To the left of the building stand the rustic servants' quarters and stables. One can't help but notice the perfectly-shaped Montaña Frontón rising up in the background of this naked setting; in fact, it's not a real mountain, but only the tail of a long ridge. The Casa del Capellán (Chaplain's House), another old and dilapidated building, sits off the side of the Corralejo road, on the left. This house, and a small house in the village, which has a stone façade with an Aztec motif, are other examples of the as yet unexplained Mexican influence seen earlier in the day at Pájara.

From La Oliva make for Lajares: take the road forking off left opposite the church, the FV10 signposted to El Cotillo.* The road runs alongside the pale green lichen-smeared *malpais* (the 'badlands') — a pleasant change in

*How are you doing for time till the last ferry? If you have an hour in hand, *do* make a 17km detour to El Cotillo (▲▲▲✕). Once there, any of the tracks leading out past the 17th-century watchtower perched on the cliffs at the edge of the village would give you a taste of the exquisite little coves ensconced in the dark lava coastline. From El Cotillo a road leads directly on to Lajares.

Molino at Valles de Ortega

the landscape. Bear right for Lajares where the main road continues left to El Cotillo — or take this detour, if you have the time.

We circle Montaña La Arena before coming into **Lajares** (177km) and passing between two roadside windmills. The one on our left is called a *molina:* a wooden contraption that rotates and is built onto the rooftop of a house. The house normally has a room on either side of the mill. On our right we have a *molino:* it's conical and is rotated by pushing the long arms, thus moving the cap with the windmill blades. This building is not inhabited. Both mills were used for grinding *gofio*. There's also a curious church nearby. Lajares is an attractive little village of white houses set amidst dark lava-stone walls.

From here it's a straightforward run back to Corralejo: turn right at the roundabout in Lajares, taking the FV109, then turn left on the FV101 at a T-junction. The Malpais de Hurimen takes us almost all the way to the outskirts of **Corralejo**, from where we follow a palm-lined dual carriageway back towards the port (190km).

Molina at Tiscamanita

 Walking

While Lanzarote may not be the destination you might choose, were you planning a walking holiday, you will be as surprised as I was to find what this island has to offer walkers and nature lovers.

The walks in this book cover a good cross-section of the island. Do them all, and you will almost know Lanzarote inside-out. Almost — because, in a very commendable attempt to preserve the beauty of the island, the government will not permit you to explore the Timanfaya National Park on your own; you'll have to join the coach-trippers or arrange a guided walk.

There are walks in this book for everyone — take your choice after reading 'Organisation of the walks' on page 49.

Guides, waymarking, maps

You won't need a **guide** for any walk described in this book — with one exception. I strongly recommend Walk 15 in Timanfaya, which you should arrange as soon as you arrive on the island; see details on page 110.

Waymarking is rare, but in some cases cairns and splashes of paint will help you find your way; these are mentioned in the text.

The **maps** in this book have been adapted from the 1:25,000 maps of the Servicio Geográfico del Ejercito. Mine are rather old and have been updated in the field. Enquire at your local map stockist if you want the latest maps of the island at either 1:25,000 or 1:50,000 — both are available.

Where to stay

Most of you will be staying in one of three places: Puerto del Carmen (the tourist capital), Costa Teguise (smaller and classier), or Playa Blanca (quiet, and conveniently located for the Fuerteventura ferries). Any of these bases is fine, provided that you have a hired vehicle. However, if walking is more important to you than is the beach, and you are not planning to hire a car, it would be best to base yourself in Arrecife, from where you can easily get to all the walks by local bus. Puerto del Carmen does have a regular bus connection with Arrecife, but

bear in mind that the service returning from Puerto del Carmen to Arrecife is not always strictly to the timetable. Costa Teguise has a limited service connecting with Arrecife, and the service between Playa Blanca and the capital only runs a few times a day.

All three tourist centres are within reach of at least five walks in the book, and you will find that by sharing a taxi one way and taking a local bus for the other part of the route (since you can usually get a bus at least one way), the cost for getting to and returning from walks is not high.

What to take

If you're already on Lanzarote when you find this book, and you don't have any special equipment such as walking boots or a rucksack, you can still do some of the walks — or buy yourself some equipment in one of the sports shops. Don't attempt the more difficult walks without the proper gear. For each walk in the book, the *minimum* equipment is listed.

Please bear in mind that I've not done *every* walk in this book under *all* weather conditions. Use your good judgement to modify my equipment list according to the season! You may find the following checklist useful:

walking boots (which must be
  broken-in and comfortable)
waterproof rain gear (outside
  summer months)
long-sleeved shirt (sun protection)
bandages and band-aids
plastic plates, cups, etc
anorak (zip opening)
spare bootlaces
sunhat
insect repellant
small rucksack

up-to-date transport timetables
lightweight water containers
extra pair of socks
long trousers, tight at the
  ankles
protective sun cream
knives and openers
2 lightweight cardigans
plastic groundsheet
whistle
compass
torch

Weather

With an average annual temperature of 21°C and less than 140mm (5½ inches) of rain per year, Lanzarote has about 125 days of sunshine. You can't go wrong on a winter holiday here.

From left to right: lampranthus and Rumex vesicarius *(dock family)
flourish near the coast; aeoniums abound from 100-800m. The ice plant*
(Mesembryanthemum crystallinum) *is another coastal dweller.*

The prevailing wind is the *alisio* — the northeast trade
wind. When this is blowing, the weather will be stable
and generally fine. You may strike a few bad days, but
the only place where the trade winds could ruin your day
would be in the north, where low cloud might prevent
you from appreciating those superb seascapes. It is very
rare for rain to disrupt an entire day on the island. It
usually lasts for only an hour or two, and then the sun
shines again — at least on the coast.

If, however, the wind swings from northeast to southwest, you are in for a few bad days. 'Southwesterlies'
invariably bring rain that covers the entire island, but they
occur rarely (and mostly in spring or autumn).

In spring and summer there are occasional days when
a warm wind blows from Africa *(sirocco)*, bringing with
it fine particles of dust. It's not very pleasant, as the temperatures can be quite high, but it only lasts a few days.

Fortunately for walkers, there are some cool and
cloudy days — these are not as uncommon as the tourist
brochures would lead you to believe. The winter months
(November to March) are best for walking, but even then
the days can be hot.

A few facts and figures: Temperatures average between
14-21°C in winter and 18-28°C in summer, with humidity
reaching between 60-70%. Good news for windsurfers:
Lanzarote is a relatively windy island, and the mean
average water temperature is 20°C.

Nuisances

Dogs should not pose any problem on the island; all
the 'working' dogs are either chained up or attended by
their owners. **Mosquitos** will keep you awake at night. so
be sure to apply ample anti-mosquito cream to keep them
at bay. There are no other nuisances on the island … of
the animal or insect variety.

But in recent years the **jeep safari** has become popular on the island, and you may find yourself eating dust on a few of the walks. Fortunately, in their frenetic search for quick thrills, they never stay in one place long enough to shatter the peace.

Spanish for walkers and motorists

In the tourist centres you hardly need know any Spanish. But out in the countryside, a few words of the language will be helpful, especially if you lose your way.

Here's an — almost — foolproof way to communicate in Spanish. First, memorise the few short key questions and their possible answers, given below. Then, when you have your 'mini-speech' memorised, always ask the many questions you can concoct from it **in such a way that you get a 'sí' (yes) or 'no' answer.** *Never* ask an open-ended question such as 'Where is the main road?'. Instead, ask the question and then suggest the most likely answer yourself. For instance: 'Good day, sir. Please — where is the path to Máguez? Is it straight ahead?' Now, unless you get a 'sí' response, try: 'Is it to the left?'. If you go through the list of answers to your own question, you will eventually get a 'sí' response, and this is more reassuring than relying solely on sign language.

Following are the most likely situations in which you may have to practice your Spanish. The dots (…) show where you will fill in the name of your destination. Ask a local person — perhaps someone at your hotel — to help you with place name pronunciation.

Asking the way
Key questions

English	Spanish	approximate pronunciation
Good day,	Buenos días,	**Boo**-eh-nohs **dee**-ahs,
sir (madam,	señor (señora,	sen-**yor** (sen-yor-ah,
miss).	señorita).	sen-yor-**ee**-tah).
Please —	Por favor —	**Poor** fah-**vor** —
where is	dónde está	**dohn**-day es-**tah**
the road to …?	la carretera a …?	lah cah-reh-**teh**-rah ah …?
the footpath to…?	la senda de …?	lah **sen**-dah day …?
the way to …?	el camino a …?	el cah-**mee**-noh ah …?
the bus stop?	la parada?	lah pah-**rah**-dah?
Many thanks.	Muchas gracias.	**Moo**-chas **gra**-thee-ahs.

Possible answers

English	Spanish	approximate pronunciation
Is it here?	Está aquí?	Es-**tah** ah-**kee**?
there?	allá?	ayl-**yah**?
straight ahead?	todo recto?	**toh**-doh **rayk**-toh?
behind?	detrás?	day-**tras**?

right?	a la derecha?	ah lah day-**ray**-chah?
left?	a la izquierda?	ah lah eeth-kee-**er**-dah?
above?	arriba?	ah-**ree**-bah?
below?	abajo?	ah-**bah**-hoh?

Asking a taxi driver to take you somewhere and return for you, or asking a taxi driver to meet you at a certain place and time

English	*Spanish*	*approximate pronunciation*
Please —	Por favor —	**Poor** fah-**vor** —
take us to …	llévanos a …	l-**yay**-vah-nohs ah…
and return	y venga buscarnos	ee **vain**-gah boos-**kar**-nohs
at (place) at (time).	a … a … .*	ah (place) ah (time).*

Just point out the time on your watch.

Organisation of the walks

The book describes rambles all over the island. To choose a walk that appeals to you, you might begin by looking at the touring map inside the back cover. Here you can see at a glance the overall terrain, the roads, and the location of the walks. Flipping through the book, you will see that there is at least one photograph for every walk. Having selected one or two potential excursions from the map and the photographs, turn to the relevant walk. At the top of the page you will find planning information: distance/time, grade, equipment, and how to get there. If the grade and equipment specifications are beyond your scope, don't despair! *There's almost always a short or alternative version of a walk,* and in most cases these are far less demanding. *If you want a really easy walk, you need look no further than the picnic suggestions on pages 11-14.* For the hardy among you, look no further than Walk 2 (and its alternative version); these will get you huffing and puffing!

When you are on your walk, you will find that the text begins with an introduction to the landscape and then turns to a detailed description of the route. The **large-scale maps** (all 1:50,000) have been annotated to show key landmarks. **Times** are given for reaching certain points in the walk. *Do* compare your pace with mine on one or two short walks, before you set off on a long hike. Don't forget to take bus connections into account!

Below is a key to the symbols on the walking maps:

LZ-3	main road	🗻	best views	⚲	pylon, wires
	secondary road	✝	church or chapel	🚗	car parking
	track	† ⊞	shrine/cemetery	🚌	bus stop
3 →	route of the walk and direction	♪	spring, tank, etc		A-A lava
3 →	alternative route	P	picnic spot (see pages 11-14)		pahoehoe lava
					grassland

1 AROUND LA GRACIOSA

See also photographs page 14 and cover

Distance: 19km/11.8mi; 6h

Grade: easy, with gentle ups and downs, but long. Can be very hot. No shade

Equipment: comfortable walking shoes, sunhat, light cardigan, rain-gear, swimwear, suncream, picnic, plenty of water

How to get there and return: 🚌 to Orzola (Timetable 8), then ⛴ to La Graciosa (Timetable 17). *Note:* the sea can be choppy!

Short walk: from Caleta del Sebo to the tidal lagoon (setting for Picnic 1) and back (2.5km/1.6mi; 45min; easy). Heading out from Caleta del Sebo turn off left for the cemetery (see map), which lies a little over 10min uphill. Then descend to the sea, bearing slightly right. In 8min, you'll reach the lagoon … if the tide is in. This is a beautiful spot to spend the day if you don't want to walk far; the return along the seashore takes about 25 minutes. Note that there's little shade.

Alternative walk: You may prefer to follow coastal paths between Caleta del Sebo and Playa del Ambar (see map) — the distance is about the same, but it's somewhat slower going. The only disadvantage is that you might stop off at one of the pretty little beaches just at the start of the walk and go no further! Just north of Pedro Barba there is a blowhole and just north of Playa del Ambar an inlet bridged by four rock arches.

All of you will have seen La Graciosa from the Mirador del Río. The vista is unsurpassed. For many people, this view from the *mirador* (shown below) is sufficient. But this little desert island deserves a second look. Take a ferry over and see for yourself. You'll discover superb beaches, sand dunes, lop-sided craters, and a lagoon. The fishing village, Caleta del Sebo, seems to be in perpetual slumber; a relaxing calm pervades.

Getting there is fun in itself. Taking the pint-sized ferry over, you pass through the straights of El Río in the shadows of the towering Famara cliffs.

La Graciosa from the Mirador del Río: the little port of Caleta del Sebo reaches out to sea, while the volcanoes of Mojón (left) and Pedro Barba (right) rise in the background. Straight below lie the Salinas del Río.

Playa de las Conchas rests at the foot of the maroon slopes of Montaña Bermeja. This clean beach of golden sand drops deeply into a blue sea.

Once you've got your legs back on steady ground again — on the quay at Caleta del Sebo, **head off** along the waterfront to the left. The village is a simple fishing haven of small low-slung houses. There are no gardens, no trees. Stark naked! At the end of the promenade, veer inland up past Bar Girasol Playa (which is also a pension). A dusty track takes you up onto a gravel road on your right. Keep on this main inland route.

Out of the houses you cross a sandy/gravelly flat area, covered in various species of salt-resistant vegetation — *aulaga* (photograph page 94), *barilla* (the 'ice plant'; photograph page 47), *Schizogyne sericea* and *Traganum moquinii*. Looking back down the track, you have a superb shot over the village clustered along the water's edge to the dramatic Risco de Famara and the striking Playa del Risco (Walk 2), curving round the foot of the cliffs. On windy days you'll curse this dusty terrain. The two volcanoes, Pedro Barba (right) and Montaña del Mojón (left), rise up ahead on either side of the track. A third, Montaña Clara (an island), soon appears in the background, centred between the other two.

At about **35min** you pass a fork off to the left around the north side of Montaña del Mojón. Shortly after, the track forks again (just in front of the village dump). Go right for Caleta de Pedro Barba. Reddish *cosco* (*Mesembryanthemum nodiflorum*; the red ice plant) brightens up the inclines here. Heading along the base of Montaña Pedro Barba, your view stretches beyond the wall of cliffs to the Jable plain and the distant volcanoes of Timanfaya. Soon you cross a low crest and descend to a lower plain, edged by short, abrupt hills. Alegranza comes into sight, rising up out of the sea into an impressive table-topped mountain trailed by a tail of hills. The remains of stone walls come as a surprise out here. What could they have grown?

At about **1h40min** come to a branch-off left — our continuation, which circles the island. But why not first visit the beautifully-kept little port of Caleta de Pedro Barba: stay on the main track and head to the right; it's only about 10 minutes away. All the fishermen's old cottages here have been given glamorous 'facelifts'. Gardens filled with palms and shrubs encircle them, and a sandy cove sits just below. The good-sized jetty, which encloses a pool, points to the fact that this is no ordinary weekend retreat — it's a lovely serene spot with a good outlook over the cliffs and to Orzola.

Continuing around the island, we head towards Alegranza on a rougher track. The north coast is sandier; dunes grow into the landscape. Ignore the faint forks off to the right within the next 15 minutes. *Polycarpaea nivea,* a dense, silvery-leafed plant, grows in the dunes. *Suaeda vera* crowns the little ant hills of sand that cover the plain. Montaña Bermeja, the 'Red Mountain', soon appears on your left, and Montaña Clara reappears, seemingly joined to the island.

At about **2h40min** the track forks; keep left and head towards the dunes to make for Playa del Ambar. What appears at first to be a lovely beach soon becomes a disappointment — it's littered with washed-up rubbish. Moreover, the rocks beneath the water's surface make swimming here awkward. The setting, however, makes an appealing photograph — the white dunes, green sea, and the volcanic hues of the mountains in the background. Don't worry — a better beach is en route! *Note: the west-coast beaches are usually treacherous; take care when swimming!*

The track heads behind and above the beach, fading as it crosses the dunes. Just after dropping down to the shoreline, we meet our turn-off, about 1h from the Caleta de Pedro Barba junction. Attention: it's a very faint track striking off left; it quickly becomes more obvious. Don't continue straight on; that way leads to Punta Gorda.

Shortly you're alongside Montaña Bermeja. The dunes lose their strength and flatten out, and Pedro Barba now reveals its crater. Further along, the Timanfaya side of Lanzarote comes into sight. Approaching the coast, you come to a T-junction (**4h**; just before a strip of sand dunes). Playa de las Conchas, the exquisite beach shown on page 51, lies just over 10 minutes along to your right. Montaña Clara stands up boldly, across the water.

From the beach, return to the T-junction (**4h20min**) and keep ahead. It's a gentle ascent over a low col littered with stones and rocks. Ignore all the branch-offs. Heading between the two craters, the Risco reappears like a green stage curtain, bringing an end to the walk. When you

rejoin the track on which you started out, turn right for the port. All the boat passengers congregate around the Marinero bar/restaurant before the boat leaves. You'll spot the bar as you re-enter the village (**6h**): pass the Pension Enriqueta and turn left.

2 RISCO DE FAMARA

Distance: 13.5km/8.4mi; 4h30min (if travelling by 🚐 3h30min)

Grade: very strenuous — a steep, gravelly descent of 400m/1300ft down a cliff face, with a possibility of vertigo for inexperienced walkers. No shade en route: the return is sheer slog. Don't attempt in wet weather. *Only recommended for experienced and fit walkers.*

Equipment: walking boots, sunhat, light jacket, raingear, swimwear, suncream, picnic, plenty of water

How to get there and return: 🚐 to/from Máguez (Timetable 6). To start the walk, enquire in advance if the bus is going on to Ye, the closest village to the start of the walk. If it is not, either alight at Haría and take a taxi to the parking place recommended in Picnic 2 on page 11, or go to Máguez and walk north to the starting point (add 1h). Or 🚐 to/from the parking place recommended for Picnic 2 on page 11.

Alternative walk: Ye — Playa de Risco — La Caleta. 15.5km/9.6mi; 5h. Equipment/access as main walk; return by pre-arranged taxi (or friends) from La Caleta. *Only recommended for experts.* Follow the main walk to the Playa del Risco (1h), then return to the crossing track. Climbing steadily to about 300m/1000ft, follow the cliffs south, sometimes over scree *(possibility of landslides)*. After passing above Punta del Roque (2h30min), the Playa de Famara will be in sight. Walk through the Famara *urbanización* and on to La Caleta. Map ends on pages 72-73.

This is a truly spectacular walk. You descend into the landscape viewed from the Mirador del Río and zig-zag steeply down the sheer Risco (cliff) de Famara. You discover that the captivating beach that sits imbedded in the lava tongue hundreds of metres below you is accessible after all! In the early morning and in the evening, this setting is no less than an oil painting. You'll probably want to make this an all-day hike, so do be prepared for the lack of shade.

If the Máguez bus is going on to Ye, alight at the junction just *before* the village. **Set out** by heading up the narrow road on the left (the coastal road that descends from the Mirador del Río). You pass through the hamlet of Las Rositas. The houses are shuttered and many of the plots lie in tired abandon. Low lichen-clad stone walls criss-cross a countryside clothed in fig trees and prickly pear.

Our first turn-off comes up after 500m/yds, soon after a roadside house on your right: you'll see a dyke (natural wall of rock) with a stone wall built into it. It's on the left. Two stone buildings, leaning up against the road, stand behind it. Take the stone-laid track off left, immediately before this wall. A stunning panorama slowly unravels, as you near the cliff-tops. You look straight out on to La Graciosa, bare of vegetation, desolate, and yet quite beautiful in the eyes of many beholders. The fishing village of Caleta del Sebo nestles around the exposed up out of the sea behind La Graciosa and, further afield, to the right, lies the hilly island of Alegranza.

When the track ends continue straight on, now descending on a rocky path. Standing on the very edge of the cliff (Picnic 2), you look along a sheer wall of rock that plummets to a flat shelf below. Playa del Risco steals your attention with its golden sand and shallow turquoise-green water. Another sight distracts you: the strangely-coloured pink and maroon (and sometimes orange) ponds of abandoned salt pans — the Salinas del Río.

The path swings down to the right of a power pylon. The view is captivating to say the least. The zigzag path demands keen attention, but no stretches of it are really vertiginous. An astonishing amount of vegetation clings to these cliffs, which harbour the richest plant life on Lanzarote. A number of very rare species, as well as nearly all the island's endemics are found in this northern massif. In and around these *riscos* you can find *Pulicaria*

The cliffs from the salt pans; see also photograph page 15.

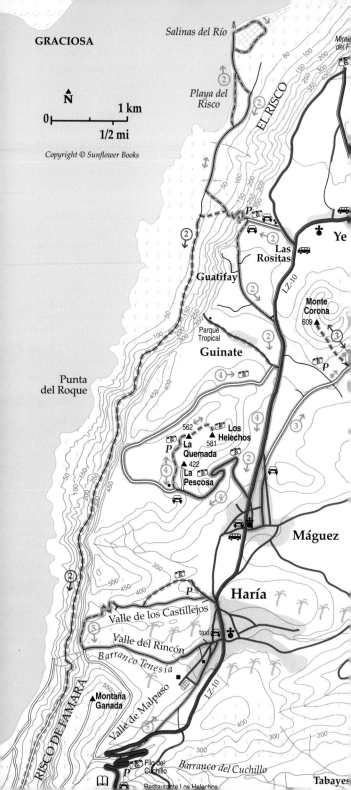

canariensis, Asteriscus schultzii, Reichardia, Kickxia, Aichryson tortuosum, two species of Aeonium, Limoniums, the rare Echium decaisnei, a yellow-flowering Argyranthemum, and many different grasses.

The desert-like Jable plain and the assortment of volcanic cones that constitute the Timanfaya National Park soon become visible over to the left. Approaching the faint track that cuts across the sea-flat below, you meet a fork: keep right. Join the track and turn right. Looking back up the way you came, you're bound to be impressed. Moreover, you know that at least here you can escape the press of tourists. Five minutes along, clamber across a dry, gouged-out streambed. Five minutes later, the track passes through a stone wall. Some 100m/yds *before* the wall, fork off left to the beach (**1h**). Nirvana! At last you can fling off your clothes (hoping that the telescope at the Mirador del Río isn't trained on you …) and plunge into the cool sea.

Now, whether you decide to swim first (*watch out for broken glass)* or explore the salt pans, your continuation is along this lovely stretch of beach. La Graciosa is just across the strait — almost within swimming distance. At the end of the beach, scramble over the stones and rejoin your track, following it to its end (by an electricity transformer station). The cliffs stand before you — a formidable barrier of rock. See if you can locate the *mirador* in the cliffs above: this will show you just how well-camouflaged it is.

From the track make your way over to the salt pans, again watching out for broken glass. Pass the remains of a derelict building (**1h30min**). Towards the end of the *salinas* you come to the second 'sight' of the walk: a magnificent pink, milk-of-magnesia-coloured pond enclosed by crumbling stone walls (photograph page 55). On a fine day you have a clear reflection of the Risco in it. On occasions the pools of the shallower pond in front of it glow a brilliant orange (see below).

We return by crossing a walkway that circles the pink ponds, cutting across the salt pan. Rejoin the track some 12 minutes back, then keep left along it. When it fades out a few minutes on, veer left uphill — you'll find it becomes clear again. Turn right at a T-junction and remain on the track for about 15-20 minutes. Some five minutes beyond the gouged-out streambed (100m/yds after crossing a small watercourse), a cairn on the left marks your ascent.

When you reach the power pylon (**3h30min**) return to your car or make for Máguez: head south on a somewhat vertiginous old path that hugs the edge of the cliff, taking in the last of this memorable view. You scale the side of a ridge running parallel with the old washed-out route to the salt pans (Alternative walk). Soon come on to a track; follow it up over the crest. Ignore all branch-offs. Descending now, the craters visited in Walk 4 dominate the Guinate Valley below you. When you reach the main road, turn right for Máguez. The plaza/bus stop lies 40 minutes downhill (**4h30min**).

The glowing ponds of the Salinas del Río

3 FROM MAGUEZ TO YE

See map pages 56-57   **Distance:** 9.5km/6mi; 3h

Grade: moderate, with ascents of about 300m/1000ft overall (of which 200m/650ft is at the end of the walk). Can be cold and misty.

Equipment: comfortable walking shoes, jacket, sunhat, raingear, suncream, picnic, plenty of water

How to get there: 🚐 to Máguez (Timetable 6) or 🚗: park as suggested in Picnic 3 on page 12, joining the walk at the 15min-point.
To return: 🚐 from Ye (reconfirm departure time before setting out!), back to Arrecife, or to Máguez to collect your car. Alteratively, telephone the nearby Haría taxi (908-64-97-14; English spoken), or walk back to Máguez (add 1h10min) for a bus or your car.

Alternative walk: Ascend Monte Corona partway through the walk (40min up; 25min down). *Only recommended for very experienced, surefooted walkers who do not suffer from vertigo; walking boots required.* The ascent starts by the second water tank, 38min into the walk. Follow the cinder track on the left-hand side of the tank. When the track ends in stone walls and terraced cactus fields, keep to the right of the fields. In some places rainwater has eroded a 'path', but basically just freewheel straight up to the top (a climb of just under 300m/1000ft). Avoid the scree; keep to the volcanic rock.

On this pleasant countryside ramble we wind our way amidst the hills of the Famara massif — the highest and (in winter) the most lush corner of the island. Farm plots keep us company. Masses of solid stone walls fortify the inclines. In spring the herbaceous slopes are flecked with dandelions, indigo *Echium,* gold-coloured *Asteriscus,* white *Argyranthemum,* and mauve and scarlet poppies. A splendid sight! The massive yawning craters of Monte Corona and La Quemada, and the neighbouring Malpais (badlands) de la Corona remind us of the volcanic origins of Lanzarote.

Our walk begins at the small plaza in Máguez, where the bus stops at an intersection. Follow the road diagonally across from you, the one that heads straight into the village. A minute along pass the colourful church square. Three minutes later, just beyond a large garden plot, turn left at an intersection. Ascending (keep straight uphill) you look back over the village, spread along a gentle valley sprinkled with palms. Some 8 minutes up, a road joins you from the right. Just past it, branch off right on a farm track lined with palms (**15min**).

You exit through hills into another valley. Keep left at the fork several minutes along, crossing a saucer-shaped valley dominated by the enormous crater of Monte Corona (609m/1995ft; photograph pages 60-61). A rough patchwork of cultivated fields stretches across the sloping inclines. Anywhere along this track is a lovely setting for Picnic 3.

Just over **35min** from Máguez we cross an intersection at the foot of Monte Corona. Notice, just past here, a water tank on the left with a blue door. Some 400m/yds past the intersection, come to a second water tank, where a cinder track crosses. The Alternative walk sets off here for the ascent of Monte Corona.

From a col 300m/yds further on, a palacial villa, the Torrecilla del Domingo, captures our attention. It sits high atop a ridge overlooking the northeastern inclines and the sea. On the slopes of Corona you see a plethora of colourful vegetation. But all colour drains out of the landscape, as we approach ash-covered fields and a vast labyrinth of stone walls. Off the hillside, keep left at a fork and enter this labyrinth.

Close to the Mirador del Río road, at around **1h05min** into the walk, the track forks. Bear left. On reaching the road, keep straight ahead (left). A gap in the crater walls above gives you a good view of its sharp-toothed crown and an uninterrupted vista over the spiky interior of the Malpais de la Corona.

At the top of the rise, where the road curves left, veer off right through a gap in the roadside barrier on a wide farm track flanked by high stone walls and descend towards the *malpais*. As the track bears right (after about 50m/yds), take the wide path straight ahead, marked by a cairn. Some 200m/yds further on, ignore a cinder track

off to the right but, 50m/yds beyond that, where a wide farm track sweeps down the hill in front of you, follow it to the right. Your route now circles another extinct volcano (La Quemada), which soon reveals a quite substantial crater. Looking back up the hillside you get a dramatic shot of Monte Corona: its razor-sharp rim rears up above the wall-rutted slopes.

At **1h35min** meet the Orzola road and turn left, continuing along the edge of the *malpais*. Some seven minutes downhill, turn left on a track that circles La Quemada. A steady, sometimes steep climb will take us up to Ye. Ignore a branch-off to the left. We sidle up against the mountain and get a glimpse of the inside of the crater. About 25 minutes off the road come to a junction: keep straight on (the right-hand fork). A deep valley slicing back into the plateau comes out of hiding. Our route dips down and crosses it. Ignore all side tracks. At **2h40min** we ascend into another, higher valley, just below the plateau, and come into Ye, a small village sitting with its back to the gaping crater of Monte Corona. Cross the road to the Mirador del Río and pick up the road heading right, into the centre. The bus stop is beside the phone box (**3h**).

Left: anywhere along the track, looking towards Monte Corona, is a good place to enjoy Picnic 3. Right: if you do the tough ascent of Monte Corona, you will be rewarded with this fine view into the crater.

4 MAGUEZ • GUINATE • MAGUEZ

See map pages 56-57

Distance: 10km/6.2mi; 3h35min

Grade: moderate-strenuous, with a steep ascent of 300m/1000ft at the start of the walk.

Equipment: comfortable walking shoes, jacket, sunhat, raingear, suncream, picnic, plenty of water

How to get there and return: 🚌 to/from Máguez (Timetable 6) or 🚗

Alternative walk: Exclude the ascent to the trig point on Los Helechos, saving a climb of 100m and shortening the walk to 2h35min.

Short walk: Los Helechos (1.5km/1mi; 1h). A moderate climb of 100m/ 330ft; equipment as above. Access by 🚗 only. Use the notes below to leave Máguez on the lane followed in the walk. Drive (on asphalt) to the white circular building and park. Pick up the notes at the 1h20min point. You'll be back at your car in 1h. Either return the way you came or, to enjoy the view shown on the cover, continue the circuit on the motorable track; you come out just above the Guinate Tropical Park.

Take it out! This summed up one reader's opinion of this walk — when it appeared as an alternative to Walk 3 in the first edition of the book. Why? Because part of the track had been asphalted, and the rest was motorable in any case. So we suggested on Update sheets that readers might like to omit this walk. And were pleasantly surprised by the response from other visitors. Not only did they urge us to leave it in the book, but to make it a walk in its own right — it's gorgeous, they said. Only

farmers use the road and track, and the carpet of wild flowers in spring is a delight. So we went to see for ourselves and decided that we could please everyone. For those of you who abhor asphalt and tracks, but have a car at your disposal, there's a delightful short walk to the twin craters of Los Helechos, from where you can enjoy one of the island's best views. But anyone wishing a longer walk, or limited to bus travel, can rest assured that this is *not* a busy road, and the only cars you are likely to see are those of the few local potato farmers.

To start out, head straight uphill from the bus stop in Máguez, following the Mirador del Río sign. Some 500m/yds along fork left up a narrow asphalted lane into the houses. As you climb, Monte Corona will catch your eye, well off to the right, but you are soon below the flanks of the Helechos volcano. About 1km along, the road curls to the left directly below Helechos, and you enjoy a fine view left down over Máguez. The ubiquitious *Nicotiana glauca* (photograph page 94) lines the road here as in so many other places on the island. Already you are approaching the fields of potatoes that characterise the higher sections of this walk.

Soon the road comes up to a rise, and the 'golf balls' atop the Peñas del Chache lie straight ahead in the south-

Climbing above Máguez early in the walk, where the road curls to the left just below Los Helechos.

A beautifully-walled potato plot marks the start of our short hike to La Quemada (left) and the trig point on Los Helechos (right).

west. Keep chugging uphill; a new crater, La Pescosa, yawns ahead on the right. Beyond a U-bend, there are fine views down over the emerald green potato plantations. A track veers off right to La Pescosa, but ignore it and make for the circular white building just ahead, reached in **1h20min**.

A cinder track turns right uphill just *before* the white building — our route to the trig point on Helechos. Even if you are omitting the climb to the summit, if you have a picnic, *do* carry on with the main walk for just a few minutes more. The track takes you up to the neatly-walled off potato plot shown above, with its own Lanzarote-green picket gate! Before you reach the end of the plot, head half-left on a grassy track/trail towards a plateau — yet another angle from which to enjoy 'the' perfect view of La Graciosa and the Risco cliffs (Picnic 4).

The main walk continues uphill to a small white building on La Quemada (562m/1845ft), past the gaping Pescosa crater on your right (the scene of a small rubbish dump). From the house make for the trig point seen ahead: keep to the left of the white building and aim for the saddle between the hill you are on and the trig point. There is no path, but your way over the grass-covered hillside is obvious. Be sure to admire the pristine farm below in the valley, with its walled fruit trees. Once on the ridge leading to the trig point, new views open up to Monte Corona and the Torrecilla del Domingo. Relax a while at the summit (581m/1905ft), overlooking Máguez straight below, with Haría beyond it and Arrieta and Mala stretching away down on the coast. Below you are twin, rubbish free craters, in line with Monte Corona. One of them is well over 100m deep, and beautifully terraced.

Return to the round white building (**2h20min**) and continue the circuit — now on a track. Eventually you descend into the Guinate Valley and will spot the Tropical Park below. You pass above the farm seen from the climb to the trig point and soon enjoy a view to the Playa del Risco, reaching out towards the port at Caleta del Sebo. The narrow strait is a turquoise mirror. A wide grassy area on the left is another magnificent viewpoint, much beloved by the local picnickers (see cover photograph). Just under 1km further on you reach the Guinate road. Head left here, to visit the Tropical Park, or go right to the main road. Máguez lies 30 minutes downhill to the right. The bus leaves from the intersection by the village plaza (**3h35min**).

From top to bottom: pimpernels (Anagallis), mauve-flowering Canarian stock (Matthiola bolleana) and yellow andryala, storks's bill (Erodium), and a tangle of white and yellow cress (Cruciferae)

5 AROUND HARÍA

See map pages 56-57; see also photographs pages 1, 15, 18, 25

Distance: 7km/4.3mi; 2h30min

Grade: easy, but sometimes slippery underfoot. A bit of scrambling through brambles. An initial descent of 220m/720ft, followed by an ascent/descent of 150m/500ft

Equipment: comfortable walking shoes, sunhat, light jacket, raingear, long trousers, suncream, picnic, water

How to get there and return: 🚌 (Timetable 6) or 🚗 to/from Haría, then taxi to the Restaurante Los Helechos

Short walks

1 Restaurante Los Helechos to Haría (2.5km/1.5mi; 1h). Easy, but slippery underfoot when wet. Equipment, access/return as main walk. Do the first half of the main walk only.

2 Haría — Valle de los Castillejos — Valle del Rincón — Haría (4.5km/2.8mi; 1h30min). Grade, equipment as main walk. 🚌 or 🚗 to/from Haría. Do the second half of the main walk only. For a *very* short walk (45min in total), leave the Castillejos Valley by the track met at the 1h23min-point and return on the far side of the valley.

Alternative walks (see also map pages 72-73)

1 Start the walk at the Ermita de las Nieves (add 3km/2mi; 40min). From Haría, take a taxi to the *ermita*, and from there follow the (motorable) track northeast past the 'golfballs' of the Peñas del Chache to the main road. Then turn left downhill for 200m to the Restaurante Los Helechos, to pick up the walk below.

2 Haría — Restaurante Los Helechos — Ermitas de las Nieves — Teguise (14km/8.7mi; 4h30min-5h). Moderate but long, with an ascent of about 350m/1150ft. Access and equipment as main walk (but take warm clothing; it can be quite cold and misty). Return by 🚌 from Teguise. Start out with your back to the town hall in Haría: turn left, then take the first left into a lane. Pass the rear entrance to the restaurant El Cortijo on your left. Keep straight ahead where a lane forks back to the right. You pass (all on the right) Cesar Manrique's former house (surrounded by volcanic stone walls), the school, some derelict cottages and the solitary old farm building shown on page 1. At the next fork, keep right. You will now climb straight up across the hairpin bends of the LZ10, the way eventually narrowing into an old stone-laid trail. When you reach the road for the sixth time, turn up left to the Restaurante Los Helechos. Pass it, and 200m/yds further on, bear right on a motorable track. Follow it below the Peñas del Chache to the Ermita de las Nieves. Then use the notes for Walk 6 from the 4h-point to continue to Teguise.

This delightful countryside ramble takes you down a centuries-old trail into the palm valley of Haría, with wonderful views all the way. After a break, you leave the village to walk up the Valle de los Castillejos, along the edge of the Famara cliffs, and then down the Rincón Valley back into the village. The ramble ends at the lively church square — the Plaza Leon y Castillo.

Pick up a taxi opposite the church square in Haría and ask the driver to take you to the Restaurante Los Helechos. Circling up the hairpins, with their impressive concrete walls, you may wonder how you're going to get back down to Haría on an 'easy' path! After enjoying the view from the *mirador* at the restaurant, **start out** by walking down the road in the direction you've just come (passing the km17 stone), with the Barranco del Cuchillo a deep gash on your right. As you approach a sharp bend, there is break in the roadside barrier on the right (just below electricity wires). Step through — into history. Stone paving underfoot recalls the days when this was the pilgrims' route from the north to the Ermita de las Nieves.

You head straight for the white 'Mirador de Haría' building on the Filo del Cuchillo ('knife's edge'). All the way down (Picnic 5a), on a very gentle gradient, you enjoy long-range views over Haría ... while you step through a veritable botanic garden. You'll cross the road (*carefully*) five times. After the fourth crossing (by a sign 'Valle de Malpaso') the way becomes a grassy track. After the fifth crossing (**30min**), the route, now a gritty cart track, initially cuts back sharp left. Around here you can pluck some wild fennel to add to your herbs if you're in self-catering accommodation. Soon Monte Corona rises just to the left of the large school building. The plots of maize, potatoes, marrows and vines are festooned with huge fig trees.

On coming to a T-junction (**40min**), head left towards the school, soon passing an old farm flanked by palms and then some derelict cottages (the latter a rare sight on Lanzarote). Coming onto tarmac, keep straight ahead — ignore the road to the left. Now watch for the house on the left surrounded by trees and lava-stone walls (just before a terrace of cottages): this was César Manrique's house at the time of his death. At a Y-fork not far past it, bear right. At the T-junction, where the town hall is on your right, turn right and immediately left, back to the taxi rank and the church square (**1h**).

Moving on (perhaps after a quick drink), follow the main street north uphill, passing a restaurant on the right. Ignore a fork back left into the village in five minutes, but at a junction a minute later, go left: pass Calle Romeiro and head downhill on Calle Casas Atraz. After about 100m/yds fork left up an earthen track with grass down the middle. Monte Corona is ahead to the right, with the green spread of Máguez below it. This delightful track through cultivation and wild flowers takes you up the Valle de los Castillejos (Picnic 5b; photograph page 18), where a dry *barranco* falls away gently on the right.

The bulk of Montaña Ganada, with its antennae, looms ahead. To the left is a series of hillocks, with neatly-

On the descent from the mirador, we look ahead to the two valleys explored in the second part of the walk.

terraced 'aprons' of vineyards. At **1h20min** ignore a track off left into fields — ahead you can see small concrete buildings — your immediate goal. Three minutes later (**1h23min**) a track joins from the right. (For a very short walk, you could turn right and follow this track across the valley and back to the main road.) By **1h30min** or less you're just below the buildings and astounded to see a row of stubby, delightfully fragrant, *shady* pines. Take a quick water break, before continuing the hike. Both the buildings and the terraces here are currently abandoned.

Leave the shade of the pines continue uphill on the track. In five minutes the track ends at a terraced plot, now given over mostly to poppies. You've climbed up to the right (north) of a castellated rocky outcrop that rises just at the edge of the Famara cliffs. Unfortunately, the coastal path below this outcrop is prone to landslides and crumbled away. You have to climb the near *(inland)* side of the outcrop and then descend to the cliff path on its *southern* side ... but there is no direct path. Still, it is relatively easy to make your own way there, scrambling uphill through the abandoned terraces (sometimes through prickly vegetation). Once up on the outcrop, take a few paces over into the Rincón Valley, and your ongoing route becomes clear. Below you there are rows of stone-wall terracing running more or less east-west, hugging the hillside, and there is a track in the bottom of the valley. Looking to the right, a single stone wall running north-south delineates the cliff-edge. Keeping to the contour on which you arrived at this view, make your way to the wall at the cliff-edge. Once there, climb over it at a convenient point and join the cliff path. (If the drops worry you, stay *inside* the stone wall, until the path widens out further downhill.)

The cliff path takes you down to the (motorable) track (**2h**), where you turn left downhill through the Valle del

Rincón — totally different in character from the Castille-jos. There are no far-reaching views, fewer flowers, and little cultivation. What catches the eye instead are the soft rosy-rusty hues emanating from the soil and the rock, set off by isolated splashes of cultivation. Notice, for instance, some 10 minutes down the track, a huge fig tree on the right, completely enclosed by a circular drystone wall. On the hillsides opposite this tree, the stone walls not only help prevent erosion, but also capture water coming off the hillside and trap it in pools — at least in spring. Two minutes later a mini-reservoir on the left allows one lucky farmer to irrigate his smallholding with hoses! Pink carnations thrive among his marrows and onions. Just past here the track is embroidered with ice plants (photograph page 47).

Looking south, you should be able to spot your descent route in the first part of the walk. A swathe of vegetation takes you back into Haría. Pass the school on the right and come into a small grove of palms, where there is a ruin ahead. Bear left in front of the ruin, then ignore a track forking back to the left a couple of minutes later. Curl around left onto tarmac. Soon a *barranco* is just on the right. At a crossroads, go straight over (after a slight 'kink' to the right). You come to the town hall and return to the Plaza Leon y Castillo in **2h30min**.

6 MALA • ERMITA DE LAS NIEVES • TEGUISE

See also photographs pages 12, 25, 27

Distance: 18.5km/11.5mi; 5h35min

Grade: strenuous, with a drawn-out ascent of 600m/1970ft in the first part of the walk. Can be quite cold, windy and misty … or even wet!

Equipment: comfortable walking shoes, warm jacket, sunhat, raingear, suncream, picnic, plenty of water

How to get there: 🚌 to Mala (Máguez bus, Timetable 6)
To return: 🚌 from Teguise (Timetable 7)

Shorter walks: both are easy; equipment as above. Take private transport (friends, or a taxi from Haría or Teguise) to start out; return by bus.

1   Ermita de las Nieves to Teguise (8km/5mi; 2h30min). Pick up the main walk at the Ermita de las Nieves and follow it to the end. If you are travelling by 🚗, park in Teguise and take a taxi from there.

2   Ermita de las Nieves to Mala (10.5km/6.5mi; 2h30min). Pick up the main walk at the chapel and use the map to walk down to Mala; it's very straightforward — but see above notes on weather conditions. If you are travelling by 🚗, park in Mala and telephone the Haría taxi (908-64-97-14; English spoken); they will collect you in Mala and take you to the *ermita;* you pay *only* for the journey between Mala and the *ermita.*

Alternative walk: See Alternative walk 5-2, page 66.

Crossing the island from east to west, we climb to the solitary Chapel of the Snows (Ermita de las Nieves) — the coldest point on Lanzarote. So if you're after some bracing air … join us and leave the sea plain! We wind up into a narrow concealed valley. The denuded clay-brown slopes soon fold up into pasture-like inclines (in winter and spring). Seascapes and mountain views accompany us all the way up to the chapel — where from a windswept plateau we enjoy a 360° panorama — the view of views.

When you leave the bus at Mala (at the *second* stop, beside a telephone cabin), **start by** heading north along

In the Valle del Palomo

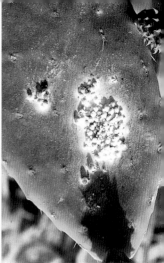

Nuestra Señora de la Merced is the little church passed at the start of the walk in Mala. Just beyond it, you come into prickly pear plantations, and have an opportunity to inspect the habitat of the cochineal insect at first hand.

the road. Several minutes along, turn off up a road branching off left — the second one you come to, where there is a road sign depicting a man descending steps. Immediately the road forks: bear right. You pass the church shown above (Nuestra Señora de la Merced). The village is immersed in fields of prickly pear — sidle up to some of these plants to see the cochineal insects thriving on the gooey white cactus juice. You can see the wall of the Presa (reservoir) de Mala ahead, wedged across the mouth of the Valle del Palomo.

In about 300m/yds we come to an intersection. The road swings left; we continue straight ahead on a rough track. Our climb begins as we leave the farmland behind. Just before crossing the crest into the Valle del Palomo, we get a good view along the sea plain of Mala, buried under a dark green cloak of prickly pear, and then the carpet of tightly-woven gardens extending back to Guatiza. Some 30-35 minutes uphill, ignore a fork right to an abandoned building. To see the fish pond-sized reservoir (the only one on Lanzarote), leave the track and cross the top of the crest; it's only a few minutes over the top.

Somewhat over 1km and 100m/300ft higher up the valley, we pass behind some houses ... and continue climbing. After gaining another 100m in height, we cross the bed of the stream, and see before us a verdant valley. After the rains have fallen, this is the most luxuriant valley on Lanzarote. Higher still, we re-cross the bed of the *barranco* and the track lazily zigzags up out of the valley. Yellow, violet and scarlet flowers set the hillside alight. Catch a corner of the Malpais de la Corona (Walk 3) over the hills. Mounting the plateau, you swing up past a Lilliputian farm dwelling leaning against a rocky nodule.

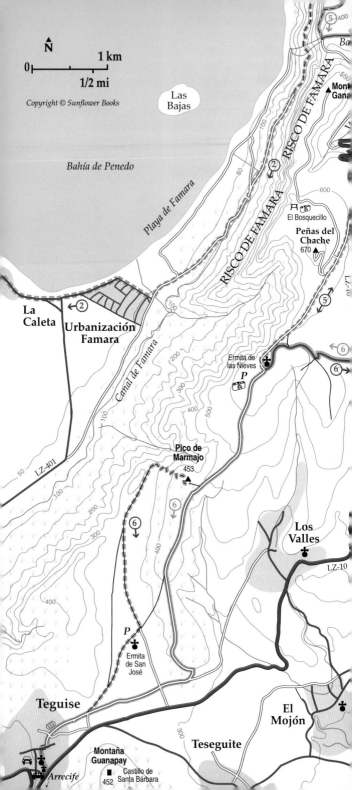

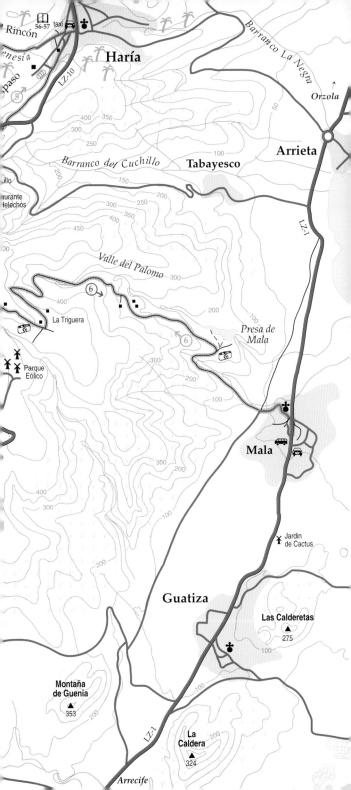

A minute or two beyond the farmhouse you circle an uninhabited house and, looking back, you have a fine view down onto Arrieta and the sea. To the northwest you see the plateau of Guatifay and the prominent cones of Corona and La Quemada (Walk 3). The great gap separating us from these craters is created by the valleys of Máguez and Haría — an impressive sight. Approaching **2h30min**, meet the LZ10 and turn left along it. Over to the right rises the island's highest summit, the Peñas del Chache, crowned by a large military installation. As you descend, the Llanos de Zonzamos (the sweeping plain behind Arrecife) comes into view, with Arrecife in the background. The refuge of Las Nieves soon captures your attention. It stands conspicuously alone on the tableland. The signposted turn-off to it comes up in 800m/yds; head right. Los Valles is visible through the mouth of the *barranco* below. Soon the roar of the sea is heard, and a roadside *mirador* gives you a view over the Playa de Famara far below.

At **3h05min** you're alongside the chapel (Picnic 6a) and probably getting a good battering from the wind. If this is the case, picnic inside the walls that enclose this haven. For an unparalleled vista, head over the cliffs *(carefully)*. Below you lies the beach of Famara. Beyond it, the desert-like Jable plain fans inland, littered with remnants

74

It's worth exploring Teguise — a jewel of a town — from all angles.

of volcanoes. On your right, the Risco de Famara (Walk 2) ends abruptly in a razor-sharp tail; beyond lie the islands of Graciosa, Montaña Clara and Alegranza.

Once you've soaked up this great view, continue on the gravel road that descends south of the chapel. It follows the crest of this declining ridge towards Teguise. The local people use this road, and the odd tourist or two will bounce past in a jeep.* Shortly the modest Castillo de Santa Bárbara becomes a prominent landmark. Fastened to the crater rim of Montaña Guanapay, it stands guard over Teguise and the encompassing plains. Following the main (motorable) track, you head back into fields. After passing a track joining from the left, you descend to an intersection (some 4.5km from the chapel). Here the track turns left to join the LZ10; however we keep straight on through the intersection. Some 12-15 minutes beyond the intersection, come to a wide track and bear left along it.

Entering the rear of Teguise, pass the stadium and come upon a somewhat confusing junction. Just keep straight on, aiming for the church tower shown in the centre of the photograph above. A street leads you down through houses and over a small bridge. Immediately beyond it, leave the street and cross an open space to the church. An arched portal lets you through into a pretty plaza. Exit alongside the Caja de Canarias (take a peep inside this excellently-restored building). You come out to another beautiful square (**5h35min**); here, outside a second church, catch your bus.

*If you don't like sharing your walk with motor vehicles, you can use the map to follow another track — marked with dashed green lines. To get there, watch out, exactly 2km downhill from the *ermita*, for a clear, sandy-coloured track on the right, leading to a small rise. Walk up the rise and look below: to the right is a very deep ravine, but straight below you is a large rectangular field. Behind the field there is a track. It's an easy scramble down to this other track, which you follow to the left. Two kilometres outside Teguise, fork right to pass the substantial remains of the Ermita de San José (see map; Picnic 6b).

7 MANCHA BLANCA • PLAYA DE LA MADERA • TINAJO

Distance: 21.5km/13.3mi; 5h20min

Grade: easy but long. Since there is no shade en route, this walk is not recommended in very hot weather. Note also: if you plan to swim in the rock pools or at the beach, make absolutely certain that the sea is safe. I have never swum at the beach myself, because it never looked safe enough to me!

Equipment: comfortable walking shoes, cardigan, sunhat, raingear, suncream, swimwear, picnic, plenty of water

How to get there: 🚌 to Mancha Blanca (Tinajo bus, Timetable 11)
To return: 🚌 from Tinajo (Timetable 11) or 🚕 taxi

Short walk: Mancha Blanca — Tinajo (6.5km/4mi; 1h45min). Easy stroll on country lanes, through beautiful farming country. Access/return as above; wear comfortable shoes and take a sunhat. Follow the main walk for 55min, then fork right for Tinajo, picking up the main walk again at the 4h30min-point. If travelling by 🚕, park at Tinajo and take a bus to Mancha Blanca to start, picking up your car at the end of the walk.

Alternative walk: Timanfaya costal path. Quite easy, but walking boots should be worn, as the entire path runs over lava. 🚕 to Playa de la Madera and return: the rough but motorable track is shown as the walking route on the map overleaf. From the beach a path runs south along the coast. Follow it for as long as you like and return the same way. This is the only place where you can wander freely inside the Timanfaya National Park. The lava formations on the coast, the views to the volcanoes in the southeast, and the mesmerising breaking of the waves make for an exhilarating hike. *See also page 118.*

This walk will not appeal to everyone. It takes you straight through the vast lava flows that have buried much of the southwest of Lanzarote. Not a soul lives out here — not even plants survive. It's a no-man's land. Deep in its midst, you stumble upon islands of lava-free ground, called *islotes* (see page 79). Here you'll find some plant life and cultivation taking refuge. It's a curious landscape that few would dare to call beautiful, but it has a special allure.

Alight from your bus in Mancha Blanca at the Yaiza/Montañas del Fuego junction, and **set off** following the LZ67, signposted to Yaiza and the Timanfaya Visitors' Information Centre. Keep right when the road forks. We skirt this well-dispersed rural village. Stone walls hedge in the road and cordon off the countryside. Here we're on the edge of a sea of 'AA' lava (a sharp, unevenly-surfaced lava; see photograph page 114). The grand crater

The dark picón-covered gardens of Mancha Blanca, with the yawning craters of Montaña Caldereta and Montaña Blanca in the background

76

dominating the scene is Montaña Blanca (see below), and pint-sized Montaña Caldereta sits in front of it.

At the T-junction less than **15min** along, head right. From here we follow tarred country lanes through fields. Seven minutes later, before a solitary house ahead to the right, turn sharp left (by a 40km speed restriction sign). The sharp colour contrast of vivid green plots and ash-grey *lapilli* enhances this picturesque countryside. Montaña de Tenezar rises up boldly at the end of the road. Another junction awaits you at the foot of the mountain, where there is a solitary farm ahead on the right, at **55min** into the walk. Turn left (*right* for the Short walk). After passing two forks off to the right, the tar peters out into a motorable track. You head into lava that now takes over the landscape. The craters of Montaña Blanca and son soon bulge up out of the lava. Up close, the mountain's rocky exterior resembles a freshly-baked cake.

Slowly, the off-shore islands appear: Alegranza, the furthest afield, Montaña Clara, and finally La Graciosa. The dark lava drops off into a deep blue sea. Without warning, suddenly the lava flow subsides and reveals a basin of low stony hillocks that lean up against Montaña Blanca like cushions. A couple of stone *casitas* can be seen, set in a coomb in the shoulders of the crater. This is Casas del Islote. We pass a fork off left to Casas del Islote and the Montañas del Fuego at about **1h45min** and dip down into an *islote*.

Some 25 minutes further on pass another turn-off to the right. From a rise eight minutes further on, you spot

the first of the beaches, Playa de las Malvas. These black sand beaches are small and the waters usually turbulent. A tiny lagoon sits back off the beach here. Beyond this playa we head back into the lava again and, less than 15 minutes later, we drop down onto Playa de la Madera (**2h35min**). This small cove doesn't look too friendly either. Play it safe and stick to the rock pools. Pillows of yellow-tipped *Zygophyllum fontanesii* (*uvilla* — 'little grapes') grow out of the sand. A path crosses the beach and climbs into the rock on the other side, from where a coastal path heads south (Alternative walk; see also page 118). Shallow and inviting rock pools (only safe when the sea is calm) lie nearby.

Some 1h55min into the straightforward return walk you rejoin the road by the solitary farm below Montaña de Tenezar. This time, keep straight on for Tinajo. La Graciosa is at last in full view, and the Risco de Famara (Walk 2) dramatises the landscape as it bursts straight up out of the sea. Tinajo is a sprinkling of hamlets that

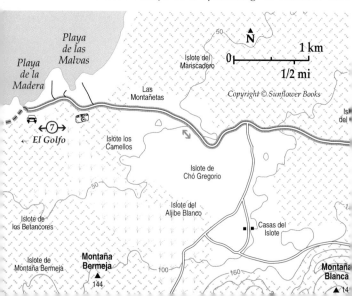

Left: waves crash on the Timanfaya coast ahead, as we near the Playa de la Madera. Right, top: curious 'islands' of greenery (chiefly tabaiba) rise out of the lava. These islotes *are patches of ground untouched by the eruptions in the 1700s. Tabaiba (middle) flourishes on the island, but uvilla (bottom) is confined to coastal areas.*

sprawls over a large cultivated plain. Entering the village, keep straight along, passing all turn-offs to the right. On reaching a large intersection, go left, taking the second of the two roads leading down to the plaza (**5h20min**). The bus leaves from outside the *dulcería* (cake shop), across from the plaza.

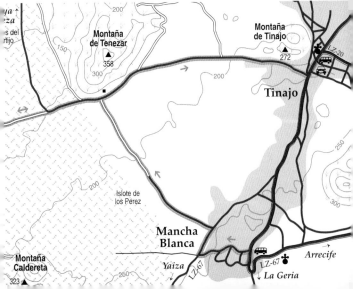

8 UGA • MONTAÑA DE GUARDILAMA • MACHER • PUERTO DEL CARMEN

Distance: 12.5km/7.8mi; 3h40min

Grade: relatively easy climb of 200m/650ft and descent of 420m/1375ft, *excluding* the ascent of Guardilama. The ascent of Guardilama involves an additional steep climb and descent of 180m/590ft, sometimes over loose stones.. The climb is also to be avoided in hot weather, but remember, on the other hand, that the peak can be very cold and windy!

Equipment: comfortable walking shoes (walking boots if ascending Guardilama), jacket, sunhat, suncream, raingear, picnic, plenty of water

How to get there: 🚐 to Uga (Playa Blanca bus, Timetable 5). This bus calls at Puerto del Carmen, so if you are travelling by 🚗, leave it there and collect it on your return.

To return: 🚐 from Puerto del Carmen (Timetables 2, 5), or your 🚗

Shorter walk: Exclude the ascent of Guardilama; this takes about 1h off the total time and makes for an easy ramble.

Note: this route is sometimes followed by jeep safaris — give them a wide berth, and they'll be out of your way quickly.

The island's farming methods are of much interest on Lanzarote. With great ingenuity the islanders have been able to grow a variety of produce. This hike takes you through the dark ash fields of La Geria — an intriguing landscape patterned by hollows and stone walls. You then cross the grassy summits that divide east and west, two quite different worlds! Here you'll see the wonders the country folk have worked with the land, and if you speak a little Spanish, they'll be only too proud to show you the way they've gone about it. The *mirador* atop

Montaña de Guardilama reveals a world of vivid contrasts: vineyards and vegetable plots, meadows and ash fields, and the great lava flows. It opens up the interior of the island for you, and you have a fine outlook over the lunar landscape of the Timanfaya National Park.

Leave the bus at the cheerful square in Uga. **Start out** with your back to the church door: head left (back the way the bus came in). Pass a games court on the left and come to a junction at Calle El Ganchillo: walk down Calle Joachín Rodriguez, then fork left into Calle La Agacha-dilla. Walk past house No 136 on the left, then turn left on Calle Los Arenales (a tarred road, just before the main LZ30 to La Geria and Teguise). Two minutes along, leave the road and climb a farm track on the right, the first one you come to. The route overlooks the village, which nestles in a shallow depression of gardens, its back to a vast expanse of crusty lava. Out of the lava rise the great fire mountains of Timanfaya, their inclines splashed with rust browns and reds. A cluster of adjoining hills stands to the south of the village. These climb into the southern massif — Los Ajaches.

The track carries us up to the Teguise road. A few minutes along it, to the left (50m/yds past the km22 stone), we fork off right onto another track heading into the hills above. We're now entering the Geria Valley. Vines and fig trees fill the small hollows. The ash fields are orna-

mented by an assortment of stone walls. Our route will take us straight over the *cumbre*, the island's spine. Ignore all turn-offs. Wandering through this black-ened world is quite extraordinary. Over to the left, the lava fields grow into a vast lake ruptured by weather-worn cones, and above us stands a line of grass-capped hills that glow with greenery. The solitary white farmsteads stand out like sanctuaries in this inhos-pitable landscape. Before long, walls take over the countryside. You're entering the vineyards, and

From the top of Guardilama, you have a superb view over the Geria Valley and to the mountains of Timanfaya.

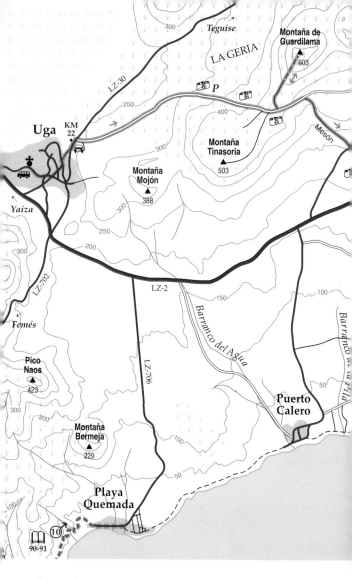

the inclines are pock-marked with depressions that are collared by half-circles of stone walls (see pages 28-29 and 80-81). We're in malmsey territory, where the well-known *malvasía* originates. This myriad of walls could be the ruins of a grand ancient city.

Crossing the saddle of the *cumbre* the way eases out. You'll have a superb view back over La Geria and Timanfaya (Picnic 8). Just over the pass, we turn off for the ascent of Montaña de Guardilama, at **1h** into the walk. We follow the faint track shown on page 84: it cuts off to the left a few metres beyond the last vineyard (some

150m/yds beyond the second branch-off to the right). Cross a grassy field, briefly running alongside the vineyards, then head straight up the mountain in front of you. When the track ends, continue straight up to the summit — a tiring climb, as it's very steep. Nearing the end of the climb, you're scrambling over loose rocks and stones (this makes the descent quite difficult; take care!). At the **1h30min**-mark you flop down on the summit. If it's a windy day, you won't be able to stand upright or even take photos up here! The panorama is, however, magnificent and encompasses the waves of hills in the south, as well as the Risco de Famara and La Graciosa and its neighbouring islets in the north. The sharp, rocky mountain crest drops straight down into a cultivated crater and out onto the pitted ash fields of La Geria. Uga and Yaiza (Walk 9) lie to the southeast.

Descend slowly and carefully to the main track (**2h**), and head left towards La Asomada. Some 400m along, leave the main track and descend another to the right (Camino del Mesón). Dropping through plots, come to an intersection (within 15 minutes) and head straight through it. Pass two turn-offs left and, two minutes later, exit onto a road (Camino los Olivos; **2h30min**). Notice the charming old house at the corner here.

Continue up the road to the left, and in two minutes turn right down Camino la Calderina; it takes you down to the LZ2 just below, where the El Pozo restaurant will be to your left. Cross this speedway *carefully,* and pick up the track almost directly opposite. Remain on this track for the next 15 minutes, keeping straight down. At the T-junction at the bottom of the track, turn left. About eight minutes later, just after rounding a bend, you could take the second turn-off left up to the main Puerto del Carmen road. (The town lies 25 minutes downhill.)

The main walk keeps straight downhill on this motorable track, the Camino Barranco del Quiquere. While the views are limited, it's preferable to the main road *and* will give us the chance to follow a pretty stretch of coast. At an intersection, cross straight over the Camino del Pozo. The track ends 600m/yds further on, at the entrance to villas 13 and 25 (**3h15min**).

Pass between the large boulders just *before* the houses, to join a footpath running along the eastern side of the Quiquere Barranco. Initially walking below the colourful villa gardens shown on page 118 and then above a lido, we follow the good coastal path 1.5km into Puerto del Carmen (**3h40min**).

The steep ascent of Guardilama begins on a faint track at the end of the last walled-in vineyard.

9 YAIZA • ATALAYA DE FEMES • YAIZA

See also photographs pages 32-33, 93

Distance: 10km/6.2mi; 4h

Grade: fairly strenuous, with a steady 425m/1435ft ascent. Can be cold and windy.

Equipment: comfortable walking shoes, jacket, sunhat, raingear, suncream, picnic, plenty of water

How to get there and return: 🚌 to/from Yaiza (Playa Blanca bus, Timetable 5), or 🚗

Short walk: Femés — Atalaya de Femés — Femés (3.2km/2mi; 1h 30min; a strenuous, but short, ascent/descent of 300m/1000ft). Equipment as above; access/return by 🚗 to/from Femés. Facing the Bar Femés, walk up the road at its left-hand side, keeping the church on your left. You will meet a brick-paved road: follow it uphill to the right. At the top of the road, where it bends right to rejoin the main road, take the earthen track up to the left (just in front of a green garage door).

Alternative walks

1   Femés — Atalaya de Femés — Yaiza (7.5km/4.7mi; 2h30min). Fairly strenuous, with an initial ascent of 300m/1000ft; the rest of the way is downhill. Access: 🚌 (Timetable 4) or 🚗 taxi to Femés; return by 🚌 from Yaiza (Timetable 5). Follow the Short walk (above) to the Atalaya de Femés, then use the map on page 88 to descend to Yaiza.

2   Walk 10 and and its alternative versions start at Femés, affording many possibilities for the fighting fit — on cooler, cloudy days!

The view from the Atalaya de Femés is best appreciated at sunrise and sunset, when shadows creep across the countryside, and the last (or first) light captures the real beauty of both Timanfaya and the Salinas de Janubio. Sitting high above the picturesque hamlet of Femés, you have the southern vista of Lanza-

Picnic 9: on the climb to the Atalaya de Femés we overlook La Degollada, a small village nestled in a tucked-away valley of the Ajaches hills.

The 'Balcón de Femés' overlooks the Rubicón plain and Playa Blanca.

rote all to yourself. On your ascent you'll often see camels grazing in one of the adjoining valleys. Nearer the summit, goats and a few sheep keep you company.

The bus drops you just before the square in Yaiza. This bleached-white village has won a number of awards for its appearance. It really is picture postcard-perfect, with its resplendent bougainvillea and graceful palms. We **start off** by taking the road to La Degollada: it heads uphill between the church and the square, to a large parking area with a restaurant. Continue uphill, past a huge plaza on the left and a beautiful park on the right (built to commemorate the the 250th anniversary of the Timanfaya eruptions). Turn left on a wide street beyond the plaza (about 50m/yds *before* the walled-in cemetery, which can be seen ahead on the left-hand side of the road). Cutting across the valley floor, you look up into a tapering valley and see the hamlet of La Degollada ensconced at the end of it. Your ongoing track, at the left of the Degollada road, is visible. When the tarmac ends at an intersection (in about 200m/yds, by a house), go straight ahead on a cinder track. Ascending the valley wall, pass a faint fork off to the left. Mount the crest just over **20min** from Yaiza, by a ruined windmill on the left. A track

coming up from Uga joins from the left; we continue up this plump ridge, which will carry us all the way to the Atalaya de Femés. In the valley over on your left you may see camels.

As you climb, the island opens up, revealing a variety of scenery. Yaiza is in full view below, its brightness accentuated by the intense green garden plots and the dark sea of lava. A barrier of volcanoes, one running onto the next, fills in the backdrop. The track divides,

Casa de Cultura at Yaiza, opposite the church, in the main square

both forks briefly running parallel; keep to the right-hand fork. Come to a fork a few hundred metres up from the windmill and bear right. Your view becomes more expansive and more rewarding — dipping down now onto Uga and stretching all the way up the dark, shadowy Geria Valley (Walk 8). Some 200m/yds past the last junction, the track forks off into three different directions. Ours is the furthest to the right. Mounting another step in the ridge, we see over the sloping plains of the east to Puerto del Carmen and Arrecife. Looking north, notice the line of three lopsided craters. The way dips briefly before reascending, and we enjoy an introductory glimpse of the Femés valley. Montaña de Timanfaya, the king of the

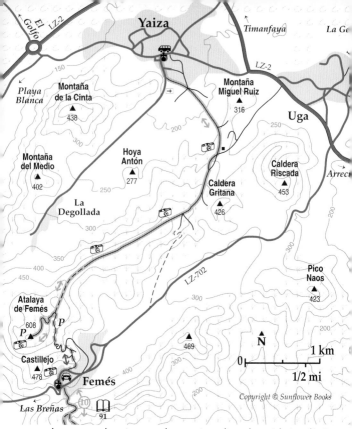

volcanoes, dominates the national park, with its distinct reddish-brown slopes.

The way fades as it remounts the top of the crest, which in turn narrows into a sheer-sided 'neck'. Another striking sight follows: the off-white salt pans and the khaki-green lagoon of the Salinas del Janubio shimmering in the sun. Scaling the final head of hills, the path briefly disappears, reappearing again to meet the Atalaya de Femés track (**2h15min**). Head right, up to the summit (608m/1995ft; **2h30min**). A stupendous view unfolds. The remote (for this island!) little village of Femés lies straight below, huddled around the pass that descends to the Rubicón plain. Fuerteventura and Lobos fill in the backdrop. And from up here you can almost count the colourful volcanoes of Timanfaya. On the far side of the transmitter station, you look down onto Las Breñas, stretching along a raised shelf of cultivation that steps off onto the Rubicón.

Allow 1h30min to return to Yaiza from the summit. In Yaiza (**4h**), the bus stop is just at the pedestrian crossing north of the plaza. (To descend to Femés and climb back up before returning to Yaiza, allow 1h15min; see map.)

10 THREE *BARRANCOS:* A CIRCUIT FROM FEMES

See also photograph page 87   **Distance:** 7.5km/4.7mi; 2h40min

Grade: moderate climbs and descents of about 320m/1050ft overall, but there is volcanic rubble underfoot for much of the walk — good ankle support is needed. Possibility of vertigo on one short stretch. The last part of the walk is a fairly steep ascent of 180m/600ft — quite a slog, as there is no shade.

Equipment: stout shoes with good ankle support (or walking boots), warm jacket, sunhat, raingear, suncream, picnic, plenty of water

How to get there and return: 🚌 to/from Femés

Short walk: Femés — Degollada del Portugués — Femés (3.5km/2.2mi; 1h35min). Equipment and access as main walk. Climb and descent of only 100m/330ft, but there is a possibility of vertigo on one short stretch. Follow the main walk to the 50min-point and return the same way.

Alternative walks (equipment as main walk; access by 🚌 private transport to Femés; return by 🚐)

1   Femés — Barranco de la Higuera — Playa Quemada — Puerto del Carmen (12km/7.4mi; 4h30min). A 10-minute climb at the outset, then a descent of 400m/1300ft (sometimes slippery underfoot), followed by some ups and downs over headlands. Follow the main walk to the goat farm (10min), then take a narrow path which descends steeply into the Higuera Valley. On the descent, looking left, you can see your ongoing route to the sea — an old washed-out track. After 30min of descent, just before an electricity pylon, fork left to zigzag down to it. Follow the left-hand side of the *barranco* down to a small beach if you want to swim; otherwise, before the beach, climb up onto the headland to find your ongoing path to Playa de la Arena and Playa Quemada (2h30min). From here a track 100m/yds inland from the coast takes you to Puerto Calero, where you can again follow a coastal path to Puerto del Carmen.

2)   Femés — Playa de Papagayo — Playa Blanca (20km/12.4mi; 5h15min; Walk 11 in reverse). Follow the main walk to the fork at the 45min-point, marked by a stone with a splash of yellow paint, and bear right. This path tends to fizzle out in goat tracks, but try to keep to the main zigzag path, or you'll have a terrible skid over the volcanic rubble. In less than 10 minutes you descend to another, smaller goat house. Ahead of you here is the dirt track followed in Walk 11. To continue to Papagayo (photograph page 13) and Playa Blanca, turn left on this track.

One of very few circular walks on Lanzarote, this ramble is ideal for motorists. If you've energy to spare at the end of the hike, why not climb up to the Atalaya de Femés (Alternative walk 9-1) to watch the sunset?

With your back to the Bar Femés on the main road, **start out** by climbing the dirt road opposite (slightly to the right), making for some ugly concrete buildings seen ahead on the hilltop. In **5min** you pass between two *aljibes* (water tanks set into the ground). Ignore a track to the right a minute later. Continue up to the buildings, and walk just to the right of the main building, still on the road/track. Looking to the left now the reason for this blot on the landscape reveals itself: there's the amusing sight

112-113

104-105

Atalaya de Femé

400

CV
LZ-2

300

Las Breñas

200

100

150

50

EL RUBICON

LOS AJACHES

50

Salinas del Berrugo

Papagayo

▲43

(11)

(10)

Playa Blanca

Castillo de las Coloradas

Punta del Aguila

Playa de las Coloradas

Playa Mujeres

Playa del Pozo

Playa de Papagayo

P

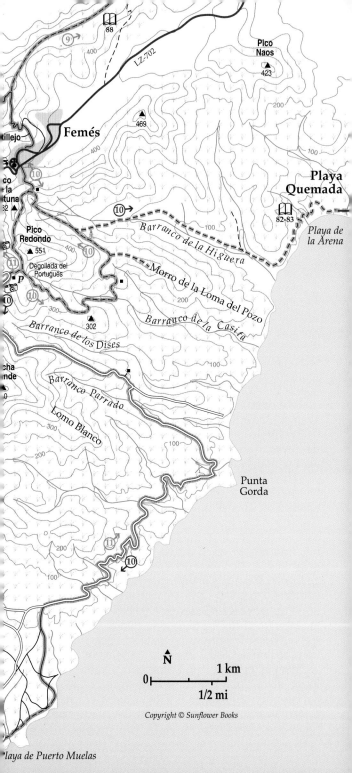

of a goat farm, and the large pen may be bursting with these delightful creatures, which are bound to keep you company later in the walk. The buildings lie at the edge of a crest overlooking the isolated Higuera Valley (**10min**) — a huge abyss, lime-green to gold in colour, due to the sparse sprinkling of grasses in the volcanic soil. Straight below you, the dry river bed traces an intricate meander in a wonderfully pristine landscape.

At this point we have a choice of two paths. One heads straight down into the valley *(the route of the Alternative walk, and the return route for the main walk).* The other heads west round the head of the valley: look to the right and you'll spot it, cut into the ledge. Walk towards it, passing to the left of another building (half sunken into the rock), and bearing slightly left downhill.

As you approach a saddle between Pico de la Acietuna ·and Pico Redondo, the way fades out over bedrock, but small stones on either side of the path keep you in line. You curl up left to the saddle and at **30min** enjoy a superb view to Playa Blanca and Corralejo on Fuerteventura. The setting is always more photogenic on windy days, when scudding clouds create an ever-changing mosaic on the featureless Rubicón plain below you. The little volcano to the west of Playa Blanca, Montaña Roja, is climbed in Walk 12; beyond it are the lighthouses at Pechiguera.

By **40min** a new *barranco* on our right drops away steeply to the hairpins of the track followed in Alternative walk 2 and Walk 11. Some people may find this short stretch uncomfortable, although our path is amply wide. Five minutes later (**45min**) be alert for a fork in the path, where a rock in the middle bears a splash of yellow paint. Our route is to the left. *(But for Alternative walk 2, bear right here.)* We climb the flanks of Pico Redondo for just two minutes, to reach a pass, the Degollada del Portugués (Picnic 10). We're above and to the left of the Payagayo track followed in Alternative walk 2. Looking below, to the right, you'll spot the small goat farm shown on page 96; Alternative walk 2 passes it. Ahead there is a wonderful view north to Puerto Calero, Puerto del Carmen and the outskirts of Arrecife. A second deep *barranco,* the Barranco de la Casita, opens out in front of us here.

Leaving the pass (and keeping an eye out for zigzags in the path), soon a third gash opens up on the right — the Barranco de los Dises. On the far side is Hacha Grande; rusty volcanic hues ripple down its flanks. Ahead is a rocky knoll colonised by an incredible variety of plants

Church square in Femés

— it stands out like a huge green *sombrero* in this hostile terrain. At **1h** we're passing just to the left of the 'hat' and walking an exhilarating ridge between the two *barrancos* — the Dises on our right and the Casita on our left. A triangulation stone can be spotted ahead ('302' on the map). The path curves to the left before this triangulation stone is reached, however. Our ongoing path can be spotted on the far side of the Barranco de la Casita, making for a stone shelter.

Descend into the *barranco*, where you'll spot a good variety of wild flowers in spring, as well as the ubiquitous yellow-flowering *aulaga* ('canary firebush', see page 94). The **1h20min**-mark sees us crossing the dry *barranco*, still making for the shelter seen ahead. The valleys glow green with wild oats and barley. At **1h30min** we're at the shelter (built in 1996), a lovely stone-built resting place with seats and welcome shade. Beside it another *aljibe* catches the rainwater off the slopes of Pico Redondo.

Head back to the U-turn in the path just before the shelter, at first going back in the direction from which you approached, then heading northeast and east — towards the Morro de la Loma del Pozo, a ridge which can be seen ahead. As you gain height, the Atalaya de Femés comes into view once more. At **1h43min** pass a path off

On the climb to the goat farm, we look back down on Femés and over to the Atalaya de Femés, setting for Walk 9 and Picnic 9.

Aulaga (Launaea arborescens; *top*) and various Euphorbias *predominate in the valleys, along with* Nicotiana glauca *(the tobacco plant, second from top). But hidden in rock crevices you'll spot many other species struggling to survive, such as yellow cut-leaf andryala and purple-flowering bugloss (*Eichium*).*

right to the top of the Morro (20min there and back). More stones line the route in this area, to keep you on course. From this angle, Pico Redondo is a smooth cone to the left.

By **1h50min** we're descending into the Barranco de la Higuera — the first *barranco* we saw from the goat house. On the far (eastern) side, the track to Playa Quemada (Alternative walk 1) stands out clearly. If you've timed your walk right, the goats will now lead you back to Femés. They'll come inquisitively (but timidly) trouping in from the slopes behind the Morro and make their way up to the farm 'for lunch' — just follow them up *(but later in the climb, when the paths narrow, please keep out of their way; they are **not** tame).*

As you approach a pylon, ruined stone walls and pens lining the path testify to a long history of goat-rearing in the valley. The paths thread out here: just walk over to the pylon, and you'll find a track which heads uphill under electricity cables. Just past the pylon, a fork heads right, to cross the valley (Alternative walk 2). We keep left, on a path between the walls and more ruined pens — following the electricity cables. The goat farm is visible up to the right.

Pico de la Aceituna is on our left now, and our outgoing path is etched into its flanks. Soon we leave the electricity wires and cross a dry *barranco*, making for the goat farm. Many 'skiddy' goat paths thread the area; if there are no goats to guide you,

just keep making for your destination on the best path —
all paths lead to the goat farm! At **2h12min** a fairly steep
dry *barranco* (offshoot of the Higuera) is crossed. Ahead,
at the top of the valley, volcanic hues ooze out of the rock
— burgundy, rust, cream, black. Ten minutes later, starting the final assault, you can either zigzag up the main
path or climb more or less straight up the bedrock near
the edge of the *barranco*. Some **2h30min** sees you back
at the farm, from where you descend to Femés (**2h40min**).

*The meandering Barranco de la Higuera, looking east into the early-
morning sun — a pristine landscape.*

11 PLAYA BLANCA • PLAYA DE PAPAGAYO • BARRANCO PARRADO • FEMES

Map pages 90-91; see also photographs page 13, 87, 93

Distance: 20km/12.4mi; 6h

Grade: strenuous, with ascents of about 500m/1640ft overall — most of it at the end of the walk. There is no shade en route, and it can be very hot, so *keep this walk for cool overcast days* — or perhaps do it in reverse (see Alternative walk 10-2, page 89).

Equipment: comfortable walking shoes or walking boots, cardigan, sunhat, suncream, raingear, picnic, plenty of water, swimwear

How to get there and return: 🚌 or 🚗 to/from Playa Blanca (Timetable 5). On arrival, arrange with a taxi to collect you from Femés at the end of the walk (or telephone from one of the bars when you arrive at Femés). Alternatively, take a taxi to Femés straight away and do the walk in reverse (see Alternative walk 10-2, page 89).

Shorter·walk: Playa Blanca — Playa de Papagayo — Playa Blanca (10km/6.2mi; 3h). Easy; equipment and access as above. If you're travelling by 🚗, you can make the walk even shorter: drive out past the Castillo de las Coloradas and keep on the tar until it ends. Park by one of the abandoned urbanizations (6km/3.7mi; 2h10min).

Sooner or later you'll discover the island's most beautiful beaches — those east of Playa Blanca, of which Playa de Papagayo is the best known. All are accessible by track, but we meander along the jutting coastline, dipping down into each of these delightful beaches, sampling them as we go. You can bet your boots they'll lure you back another day. With the last of the beaches behind you, you're unlikely to see another soul, save for a goatherd. The landscape is sliced up by ravines and hidden valleys, shut off from the rest of the island by a wall of high hills.

An eyesore of unfinished urbanizations chewing up

Walks 10 and 11: near the Degollada del Portugués you overlook the winding track to Papagayo running below Lomo Blanco on the flanks of Hacha Grande.

the coastline takes up the first half hour of our walk; they were never built due to a moratorium on building in 1994, but their roads and derelict street lamps scar the landscape.

Start off by following the coastal promenade east from Playa Blanca, making for the circular tower on the headland. You reach this well-restored tower (Castillo de las Coloradas, bearing the date 1769) in **30min**. Off this headland you have a good view back to Playa Blanca and towards the superb beaches scooped out of the open bay on your left which culminates in the Punta de Papagayo.

From here a wide path follows the coast past the large *urbanización* wasteland (where you should park if you come by car). Then another short promenade takes you to the Playa de las Coloradas. This stony beach is the ugly duckling of the *playas*. At the end of it a path takes you up (with a slight scramble) to the sea-plain above, where you find a clear path over to Playa Mujeres. Low spiny *aulaga* lies scattered across the plain. Wherever you find *aulaga* there's usually *cosco* nearby. *Cosco* (the red ice plant) turns a vivid wine colour under drought conditions, and great colonies of it stain the inclines. Its fruit was used to make a substitute gofio (normally a roasted corn flour), and was used as a thickening agent in soups, etc.

Some **1h05min** into the walk the unspoilt Playa Mujeres is in sight. This lovely open beach stretches across the mouth of a shallow *barranco*. El Papagayo, the only sign of civilisation out here, is the handful of derelict buildings near the point. Your path drops down into a small gravelly *barranco* and mounts a faint track which leads you down onto the golden sandy beach. You look back into the windswept hills of Los Ajaches. Near the end of the beach, scale the sandy bank to remount the crest — a steep, slippery three-minute climb on sand, followed by loose gravel. Continuing along the top of the crest, you dip in and out of small *barrancos* which empty out into concealed coves below.

Playa del Pozo is the next of the larger beaches. Straight after crossing a track, you clamber down a narrow streambed to reach it. Ascend the goats' path that edges around the hillside at the end of the beach, and once again you're above the sea. If the way appears vertiginous, scramble up onto the plain straight up from the beach. Now more enticing coves reveal themselves. Most days you'll find they're occupied; this coastline is well and truly 'discovered'. Soon the old settlement of

Papagayo reappears on the crest of the ridge ahead; its crumbled stone buildings leave one assuming that it's uninhabited. Circling behind a couple of coves you reach the top of the crest (**1h45min**) — and find that, to the contrary, El Papagayo *is* inhabited ... by hippies. A rust-brown and deep mauve-coloured rocky promontory separates the two dazzling coves on either side of you. From here you have a striking view of the smooth-faced inland hills, as well as along the string of beaches you've just visited (see photograph page 13). If you're only doing the Short walk, you'll have plenty of time to sample these paradisial beaches and coves (Picnic 11); otherwise, you'll only have time for a couple of them.

Continuing on, follow the path curving around the walls of Playa de Papagayo. You look down onto the beach and a number of tents fastened to the face of the hill. Ice-plants and *cosco* patch the slope. (If this path looks unnerving, make your way around via the top of the crest.) Shortly meet a track coming in from your left and follow it out to Punta de Papagayo. It passes a pillbox a couple of minutes along and then swings sharply back left. The point is just beyond the shelter. Don't go too near to the edge of the cliffs on windy days! Fuerteventura is now closer than ever, and the dark 'pimply' island of Lobos is made more prominent by the sand dunes of Corralejo in the background. Back to your left you can see Puerto del Carmen and Arrecife — a vast expanse of white trimming the sloping sea-plain. A staggered chain of cone-shaped hills runs down the centre of the island.

A few minutes below the pillbox (at about **2h**) the track fizzles out onto yet another beach — Playa de Puerto Muelas. This secluded beach is the most popular out here. Could the fact that it's the (unofficial) naturist beach have something to do with it? Five minutes along the beach (trying not to look left or right), reach the car park. Follow the track north to the next cove, a minute over, and then ascend to the top of the cliffs beyond it. Bits and pieces of track lead you along these cliffs. Some 15 minutes from the last beach you come onto a clearer track and overlook a rocky cove set at the mouth of a deep ravine. Here we turn up left, keeping straight up (bear left at the fork you encounter and pass through an intersection), until we meet a T-junction (at about **2h45min**).

Turning right at the junction, we now sidle along the hills, disappearing further out 'into the sticks'. No more beaches, no more people ... but perhaps a goatherd and a handful of goats. Ignoring all tracks that fork off left and right, we remain on an almost even contour. Gradually ascending, we look straight off the sloping shelf onto the sea. The way curves back into a number of *barrancos* that slice inland. Some **3h30min** en route, drop down into a good-sized gulley and cross a wide gravelly streambed. The countryside can be surprisingly green out here in winter and spring. Still no sign of life, nor any trees … a desolate spot indeed.

Tías comes into full view, its elevated slopes speckled with white buildings. The surrounding hills have subsided into a gentle rolling landscape. A brief descent takes you down to another *barranco* crossing. Now the hard work begins — a climb of over 400m/1300ft lies ahead. We wind our way up into the largest of the valleys so far encountered, the Barranco Parrado. Dandelions and *Echium* add their golds and purples to the greenery if you walk in spring. Some seven-eight minutes uphill from the streambed crossing, come to an junction and head left. Several minutes later, you'll see a shepherds' crumbled outpost on a rocky outcrop above the track. On a windy day it's a good picnic shelter. There's also a large colony of ice plants here. This plant was once traded for its soda content. Pico Redondo (551m/1800ft; Walk 9) is the peak rising over on your right, between the Casita and Higuera *barrancos*. Soon you encounter the first trees — some rather scrawny examples of *Solanaceae* (the tomato family) — scattered along the side of the track.

A fantastic viewpoint (where you're often hit by a gale-force wind), awaits you when you reach a pass below the Degollada del Portugués (**5h**). A small goat farm sits nearby. Make your way to it, then climb the slippery slope behind it (there *is* a zigzag path here, but a myriad of goats' trails have nearly obliterated it). In five minutes you'll come to a fork, but you may not notice it. The path heading sharply back to the right is the route of Walk 10. Keep straight on, with a steep *barranco* hard on your left, as you round the flanks of Pico Redondo. By **5h50min** you'll stagger up to a large goat farm — a great photo opportunity! Turn down left on a track before the largest of the buildings: Femés is below you. It doesn't matter if a taxi is waiting or not — collapse in the bar at the 'Balcón de Femés', overlooking the Rubicón plain (**6h**), and enjoy a drink while watching the sunset.

12 MONTAÑA ROJA

Map pages 104-105

Distance: 2.5km/1.6mi; 1h (by bus add 5km/3mi; 1h15min)

Grade: an easy climb/descent of 130m/425ft, but the volcanic pumice underfoot is slippery. An ideal walk for those with children. No shade.

Equipment: comfortable walking shoes with ankle support, cardigan, sunhat, suncream, water

How to get there and return: 🚗 to the roundabout outside Playa Blanca, then take the road for 'Faro de Pechiguera'. Beyond the Corbeta Hotel on the left (about 1km from the roundabout), turn right for 'Los Riscos'. Pass the roads left to Los Riscos, then fork left for 'Montaña Baja'. Park near the easily-seen path up the crater, not far below the relay station. Otherwise: 🚌 to/from the roundabout outside Playa Blanca and follow the notes for motorists above

Whether you're staying at Playa Blanca or just driving through, here's a short leg-stretcher to start or end your day. Montaña Roja is just a little pimple of a volcano, but in spring wonderful miniature gardens of wild flowers flourish in the pumice, and because the mountain stands in isolation on the Rubicón plain, you have very wide-reaching views.

From the parking place **start out** by climbing the path up the volcano. It's only **10min** up to the rim, where you can go either left or right. (For Picnic 12, you might like to turn left and reach the trig point in 10 minutes.) We

choose right, soon passing a path into the bottom of the crater, only 20m below. The crater floor is disfigured with 'graffiti' — small stones arranged to spell out the names of previous visitors. As you round the basin, a network of abandoned roads comes into view — one leading to the huge white Atlante del Sol building in the northwest, a landmark on Walk 13. It stands isolated in a desert wilderness.

In abut **40min** or a little more you will reach the trig point, the highest point of the walk (194m). From here there's a fine view down to the lighthouses at Pechiguera and over to the dunes of the natural park in the north of Fuerteventura.

You'll be back at the junction in another 10 minutes and down at your car in **1h**.

Rounding the small crater of Montaña Roja, you look down to the lighthouses at the Punta de Pechiguera. In the immediate surroundings are 'rock gardens', where plants like wild geraniums and leaf-lichen (Ramalina bourgeana) flourish.

13 LA HOYA • EL CONVENTO • LA HOYA

See also photograph page 118   **Distance:** 11km/6.8mi; 3h45min

Grade: moderate; the terrain is mostly level underfoot, but you're floundering over uneven lava for much of the way. The final descent to El Convento is vertiginous and dangerous if wet (but this may be omitted).

Equipment: stout shoes with grip or walking boots, sunhat, suncream, cardigan, raingear, picnic, plenty of water, swimwear

How to get there and return: 🚌 to/from La Hoya (Playa Blanca bus, Timetable 5). If you are travelling by 🚗, there are several places to park (see map). The best choices are the large *mirador* on the west side of the Salinas de Janubio (from where you can walk across the dyke separating the salt pans from the lagoon) or behind the water desalination plant — a large isolated dark yellow building off the CV (old road), 2.4km south of the El Golfo roundabout, and start and end the walk there.

I f you're tired of picnicking at the beach and eating sandwiches 'à la grit', then this coastal walk, with its superb unvisited rock pools, may be just what you're looking for. Beyond Playa de Janubio you follow a jagged, rocky coastline. There are no more beaches (or people), only natural rock pools — pools to suit all the family — hidden on the lava shelves that jut out into the sea. El Convento is the name given to the impressive sea cave at the end of the walk. It's a beautiful stretch of coastline, only frequented by the local fishermen.

Leave the bus at La Hoya (the junction for Las Breñas and El Golfo) and **start the walk:** follow the CV road south to the Mirador de las Salinas turn-off, less than **10min** along. It's the first track forking off to the right. Head out to the *mirador* — a point that hangs out over the salt pans and lagoon. From here you have a bird's-eye view over the multitude of tiny white squares of salt and the evaporation ponds that divide up the basin floor, leaving it with a sunset-pink glow. The dark green lagoon enhances this fine setting, shown on page 106. This particular *salina* (salt pan) produces one-third of Lanzarote's salt. Ornithologists will be happy to know that this is a popular destination for migratory birds as well, and you can expect to find: teal, the cattle egret and little egret (on rare occasions); the grey heron and storks (from time to time); plovers, lapwing, and sparrow hawks (more commonly). Notice also the few derelict windmills down in the basin; these were used for pumping the seawater into the ponds.

The top of the plateau is bare and dusty. From above the lagoon we continue further south, circling the top of the basin. When you come to the edge of a small but deep ravine (a few minutes from the *mirador*), clamber down the steep rocky face at its mouth. Take care, it's gravelly. A short descent (possibly on all fours) drops you down onto the basin floor, near the lagoon. Follow the track over to your left to leave the basin. You'll pass by a shed and below a house, to go through a chained barrier. Come onto the beach track at **30min**. Playa de Janubio sweeps around the shoreline below you. From here we head south (left) along the edge of the sea plain, following trails the fishermen use.

Our continuation is a very faint track that lies across the beach track. It begins a minute uphill to your left. Soon you'll see the remains of the old Playa Blanca route — a raised stone-built piece of road — below you. Keep close to the sea, so that you don't miss any of those alluring *charcos* (pools) and, where possible, scale down over the rock to check them out. You'll soon discover one that will steal an hour or two of your time. Your own private pool, too!

On our outgoing leg, we follow paths the fishermen use, floundering over rough lava, so as not to miss any of the allluring rock pools. The return, on earthen tracks just inland from the coast, is far easier on the feet.

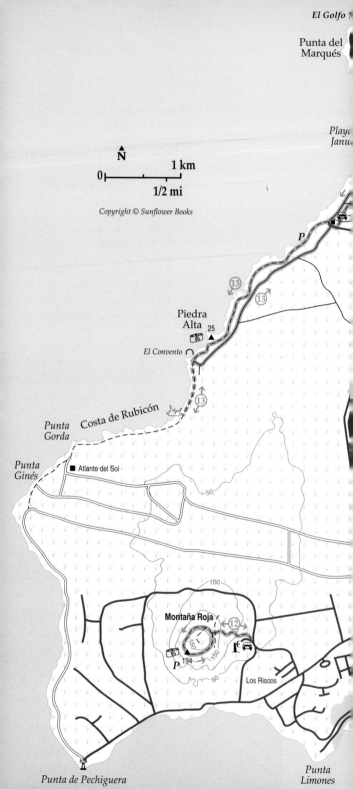

Along modest cliffs, you follow paths or just plough over the loose lava, and now and then you join up with a stretch of track. If you tire of floundering over all this rocky terrain, head inland for a couple of minutes and follow the main track (the return route), keeping parallel with the coast. Soon you're looking straight across the stone-strewn Rubicón plain to the pointed Ajache hills. In the distance, further along the coast, the water desalination plant and the abandoned *urbanización* of Atlante del Sol bare themselves. Las Breñas is the village you soon see strung out along the edge of an elevated plateau that steps back off the Rubicón. The landscape is still and lifeless, and without a drop of colour.

At **50min** into the walk you pass a wooden cross, and in under **1h** you walk behind the water desalination plant. Stretches of the coastal lava resemble cobble-stone paving. About 10-15 minutes beyond the water plant you begin finding the best pools (Picnic 13). So keep an eye out for them. The sea churns up against the shelf, replenishing these pools: obviously, swimming isn't recommended in bad weather or when the sea is rough.

At **1h10min** spot a sea-shelf (from the edge of the plain) with a number of pools embedded in it. A few minutes' scrambling over rocks and boulders brings you down to them. This is an excellent spot for children, and the pools are also deep enough for adults. Some eight minutes later, there is

another vast shelf with more inviting pools. Finally, a few minutes past this spot, you will find a magnificent solitary pool. All of these emerald-green waterholes are simply irresistible…

Attention is needed at about **2h10min**: shortly after turning inland (behind a small 'dip') to avoid a mass of lava rock, we pass a round white concrete trig marker that stands on a point to our right. Here we scramble over

Above: rock pools (charcos) *lie all along the route, and make delightful swimming holes, many of them suitable for children. Below: the Salinas de Janubio, where the walk starts and ends.*

all the rock, to the top of the cliffs, for a dramatic coastal overlook. Two inviting green pools lie in what appears to be an inaccessible shelf, immediately below. Behind the pools stands an enormous cave — El Convento — with a 'cloistered' entrance opening back into the face of the cliff. A smaller cave sits to its right. Now the problem is: how do we get there?

The safest way down is just beyond the second cave, some four to five minutes round the top of the cliff. You pass over some interesting rock formations, resembling large fragments of broken crockery. Straight off this area of rock, you drop down onto 'lumps' of lava. Metres to the right (and close to the edge of the cliff!), a nose of rock reveals itself. Locating it requires a bit of scouting about. Descend here *with care!* All fours are needed, and this descent is only recommended for very surefooted walkers! Also note: before venturing down, make sure the breakers aren't crashing over the shelf! When the sea is calm, there is no danger.

This is a superb and sheltered spot at which to spend the rest of the day. A blow hole lies a further 20 minutes along the coast, if you can summon up the energy. It's more noticeable for its noise than the spray of water. Find it on a sea-shelf set in the 'U' of the next bay along. The noise gives it away.

The return section of the walk is much easier on the feet: we follow a track that lies just a few minutes back from the top of the cliff — slightly inland from the path. Heading back, you get a good view of the Golfo crater — a prominant orange-coloured cone that rises up off the seashore. Remain on the track, keeping along the coast. Ignore all turn-offs inland. You'll cross several other tracks. By **3h** you should be passing the water plant. Just before the beach track you'll be traipsing across a rocky hillside. Above the Playa de Janubio, continue up the track to the right and, on the main road, turn left to the junction for La Hoya and your bus stop (**3h45min**).

14 MONTAÑA CORONA

Distance: 8km/5mi; 2h30min

Grade: moderate, with an ascent/descent of 235m/770ft. Some slippery terrain underfoot. Avoid very windy days.

Equipment: walking boots, cardigan, sunhat, suncream

How to get there and return: 🚌 (Timetable 1) or 🚗 to/from Costa Teguise

There's more than one Corona volcano on the island! Less famous than its brother, Montaña Corona on the northern outskirts of Costa Teguise affords a wonderful 360° panorama from the top, stetching from the mountains in the north of the island all the way across the strait to Fuerteventura. It's a typical 'collapsed' volcano, with the side towards the sea missing. So you can climb one arm of the arc, stride along the ridge, and descend by the other arm.

For those based at Costa Teguise, this hike is on your doorstep. You can see mountain from most parts of the resort. **Start out** along any of the obvious roads and join the Calle de la Atalaya which snakes around the north side of the very large Hotel Beatriz. (You can cut through to it via the Ciudad Jardin development.) At the highest point of the Calle de la Atalaya, before it bears left at the foot of the mountain, branch off across rough ground in the direction of the main peak. Head for a gap in the corner of a drystone wall. Keep on the clear path through the gap and past a large cairn. After a further 100m/yds you come to a junction. You *can* go straight on up to the top here, but it's preferable to turn right and do the walk in an anti-clockwise direction.

Having turned right, the track stays level for a bit, then dips into a relatively green little corrie. It carries you to the start of the northeastern arm of the crescent. The sharp left turn leading up to the ridge is indicated by another cairn. Now just climb the ridge, pausing to admire the views over the wild coastline, and to get your breath! Note the odd bits of plant life somehow clinging to life in the cindery rubble; the begonias grow to a maximum of 15cm here, whereas only a few kilometres away, down on the coast, they grow to over 2m/6ft in sheltered, well-watered spots.

The view from the top of the ridge is splendid — encompassing volcanic cones near and far, the distant wind generators to the north, the green 'sausages' of the golf course sitting in the gravy-brown lava, the massive network of drystone walls, and the white villages and specks of farmhouses. Arrecife, with its dominant new power station, seems only a stone's throw away.

The half kilometre walk along the curved ridge is easy in calm wea-

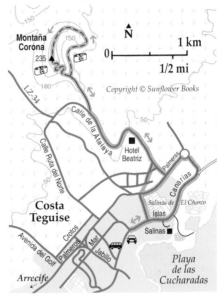

ther: although the land falls away steeply on both sides, the top is wide. In windy weather it is more difficult to keep one's balance, and it may be easier to keep a few feet below the highest part of the ridge, on the leeward side. The 'high point' of the walk, both literally and meta-phorically, is the southern end of the crescent (**1h 30min**).

The descent is very quick: just head back to the gap in the wall. There is no path at first, but the way is mostly over bed-rock and fairly easy. Lower down it's rather gravelly and slippery under-foot. You can be back on the beach in less than an hour from the summit (**2h30min**).

Top: rock formations on the ridge. Bottom: from the gap in the wall at the start of the climb our ascending and descending paths are visible.

15 TIMANFAYA — THE TREMESANA ROUTE

Distance: 3km/2mi; 2h walking (but allow about 4h)

Grade: easy, level walk

Equipment: stout shoes, cardigan, raingear, sunhat, suncream

How to get there and return: 🚗 to/from the Timanfaya Visitors' Centre, just west of Mancha Blanca on the LZ67

Note: this is a guided walk and must be booked in advance **and re-confirmed** 24 hours before the date arranged. Since you may have to wait for up to a week for a place, it's advisable to book as soon as you arrive on Lanzarote — either call in at the Visitors' Centre personally, or telephone (840839; English spoken).

There's only one walk you can do in Timanfaya on your own — the coastal path north of El Golfo to Playa de la Madera (see page 118). But this doesn't take you into the heart of the volcanoes. *Do* try to do this walk — and as early in your visit as possible. You will learn so much that will add to the pleasure of the rest of your stay — after you have learned to 'read' the landscape. Not only are the guides schooled in vulcanology, but they can answer many more questions besides!

You may wonder why visitors are not allowed to walk freely in Timanfaya. There are several reasons. Firstly, some of the lava 'tunnels' have a very thin crust — your weight could collapse them, leading to a nasty accident, far from help. A second reason is a matter of aesthetics! The park is picture-postcard perfect: the rolling volcanic slopes all appear to be dusted with a smooth coating of caster sugar — a *pâtisserie* of pristine, freshly-iced cakes. But just one footprint in this sand changes its colour, and can take three years to disappear! It

It's exhilarating to enter the national park on a clear day, when the Fire Mountains glow red above the sea of jagged 'AA' lava.

would take the wind *hundreds of years* to smooth out jeep tracks. But the single most important reason is conservation. It can take lichen — the first of the vegetation, on which all subsequent growth depends, up to *900 years* to take hold. (Timanfaya is one of the best areas in the world to study lichens: they can be seen evolving on the naked rock in extreme conditions of heat and cold, their only source of moisture the water in the rock itself and the humidity of the northeast trade winds.) Some tiny lichen which you might not even notice bear hairs that provide life-giving moisture to the animals and birds which survive in the park. Lichens grow most readily on relatively flat surfaces (where they can trap the greatest amount of moisture; see photograph page 114) and in the crevices of northeast-facing slopes, where they catch the moisture off the trade winds.

Your day starts by assembling at the Visitors' Centre at 10 o'clock. The maximum group size is seven people, and usually there are two groups. Each starts at one end of this linear trail, and the drivers exchange minibus keys halfway along the walk. (In the rare case where there is only one group, you will do only half the walk — or, if you are all strong walkers, you will do the entire route

and return the same way — 6km; your guide will decide which is best.) On the outward or inward trip, you will travel via Yaiza, where your guide will point out two old houses that survived almost six years of eruptions beginning between nine and ten o'clock at night on September 1st, 1730. (Nearby is a raised water tank with a large tilted 'apron' surface to collect the water — a *mareta*. The actual tank below is much smaller than the 'apron'. These are less common than the *aljibes* — sunken water tanks with flat roofs.

How could some houses have survived and, more surprisingly, why was no one killed in the eruptions that obliterated 14 villages in what once was one of the most fertile areas on the island? Probably because the first material vomited out was 'AA' lava, which moves very slowly; families were able to load up their camels and get away. In an eruption, three types of lava spew out: *lapilli* (fine ash), *malpais* or AA type lava (scoria), and 'bombs'. Bombs are solid and hard; they fly on average 30 to 300km away from the volcano. Bombs can be tiny (you'll be given one to examine) or huge.

If you start the walk from the Yaiza (east) end of the trail, Tremesana will be the first volcano you come to. You will see many fig trees here, most of them encircled by drystone lava walls. All this land was once private; now the national park has an arrangement with the farmers: the trees remain in private hands, but the farmers are obliged to use certain paths to reach their plots. The venerable old fig tree in the photograph on page 115 has a circumference of 12m — almost 40ft!

A very strange construction stands near the fig trees: a scoria-walled enclosure with a 3ft-high 'bed' of *lapilli* on top. What on earth could it be? Called a *pasero,* it's for drying the figs. Since scoria is full of holes, air can circulate all round the fruit. And on the subject of lava walls... those in this part of the park were built about 100 years ago by the men who built the walls in the Salinas de Janubio — 'master stonemasons', who can build a fairly high drystone wall using just one thickness of rock. (Try it yourself on one of your other walks — goodness knows but there's plenty of rock around to play with...)

The colours in the rocks are dazzling. And they vary enormously depending on their mineral content. Red

Copyright © Sunflower Books

comes as no surprise, but the sapphire-blue to mauve hues are particularly striking. Look at an example, as in the photograph on page 114: you're likely to see that one part of the rock has been formed beneath the earth and another has been formed in contact with the air — this is often evident from the shape. The part that solidified underground comes out almost black, but the part that came into contact with the air is more red from oxidisation. Some rocks are blue from cobalt mixing with oxygen and others gold from sulphur. (The guides even claim to know which way the wind was blowing during the eruption, from the colour of the hillsides! They are likely to point out a cone with yellow streaking on only one side — indicating both the wind direction *and* a second passage of sulphurous wind as the rock cooled, which makes the gold colour even paler.)

Caldera Rajada ('Split Mountain') lies north of Tremesana. If you thought volcanoes always 'blew their *tops*', then this one comes as a surprise. It split its *side,* and the resulting volcanic tube *(jameo)* reaches out just to the edge of our path. When tongues of lava flow from the point of eruption, they drag along the surface of the ground. The surface lava cools rapidly and solidifies, but molten lava (magma) continues to flow beneath the crust. The magma sinks gradually (either because the eruption ceases or because the flow follows a natural depression). Thus a cavity or 'tube' sometimes forms beneath the crust and the depressed lava flow (see photograph page 114). Volcanic tubes vary in size — this tube from Rajada formed inside and over a *barranco* and is very high. The ceilings of tubes vary greatly in thickness, too: some are very thick, while if you tap the tops of others, you'll hear how hollow they are! (At the end of the walk you'll climb inside a tube and see the 'stalactites', where the lava

Top: the vivid colours in the rocks are due oxidation. Middle and bottom: it's easy to recognise the difference between jagged AA (malpais) and smooth pahoehoe lava. One type of pahoehoe lava is called 'ropey' for obvious reasons (middle). The solidified crusts of pahoehoe lava eventually break up into great blocks, sometimes revealing the underlying tubes.

dripped as it cooled.) The famous tubes at the Cueva de los Verdes and Jameos del Agua resulted from the eruptions of Monte Corona (Walk 3).

Near the end of the walk you pass Montaña Encantada ('Enchanted Mountain') ... a cartographic misnomer. The fig farmers in the area paid a watchman to sit atop this mountain and sing out *('Canta!')* if anyone was stealing their fruit, so the mountain became known locally as

Top: this massive fig tree at the foot of Montaña Tremesana is still privately farmed: an arrangement between the park auhorities and the owners of the land permits them to work their plots, but they must use agreed paths. Middle: after a long day carrying tourists, these camels are making their way home via Yaiza. Bottom: silky-sided craters rise from a sea of jagged scoria.

Montaña Canta. But the map makers were from Madrid… Around here you will pass terrain where *malpais* and *pahoehoe* lava intermingle; their different surfaces make them instantly recognisable. There's a 'bubble' on show, too: called a *hornito*. You'll see other *hornitos* at César Manrique's house in Tahiche or if you do the walk around Lobos (see page 119). The walk ends at Pedro Perico, from where you minibus back to the centre.

16 COASTAL WALKS

My favourite coastal walks are described in full in the book (Walks 2, 11 and 13 and their alternatives), but there are many others to be enjoyed — especially if you can arrange transport, since they are all linear. Here's a selection, with approximate walking times, grades and suggestions for access. You won't need a map beyond the touring map — just follow the coast and use common sense when you encounter a property or *barranco* to be negotiated. With the good coastal breezes, these hikes can even be done in summer, but remember to *always* wear protective suncream and clothing (as well as stout lace-up shoes), and to take plenty of water! We start at the top of the island and work our way clockwise:

ORZOLA TOWARDS PUNTA FARIONES AND BACK
Distance: up to 2.5km/1.5mi; 50min
Grade: easy at first, but readers (1999) say the cliff path is now broken by landslides and *eventually becomes unsafe;* you must be sure-footed.
Transport: 🚌 (Timetable 8) or 🚗 to/from Orzola

From the ferry terminal, walk up the coastal road to the end. Then follow sandy tracks through the lava, heading diagonally towards the cliffs. When you approach Playa de la Cantería, you will see the old cliff path to Punta Fariones ahead. Follow it as far as you can, then turn back.

LOS COCOTEROS TO COSTA TEGUISE
Distance: 9km/5.5mi; 2h30
Grade: easy, but you must be sure-footed
Transport: 🚌 (Timetable 1) or 🚗 to/from Costa Teguise; then 🚗 taxi

The lighthouses at Pechiguera

from Costa Teguise to the salt pans at Los Cocoteros to begin

Ask the taxi driver to set you down just before the salt pans, where the main road turns left to the *urbanización* and a wide earthern track, shown on the touring map, forks off to the right (south). Follow the track — later a wide path — back to the Avenida de las Islas Canarias at Costa Teguise (map page 109).

PLAYA QUEMADA TO PUERTO DEL CARMEN

Distance: 6km/3.7mi; 2h

Grade: fairly easy, with minimal ups and downs

Transport: 🚌 (Timetables 1 and 2) or 🚗 to/from Puerto del Carmen; then 🚕 taxi from Puerto del Carmen to Playa Quemada to begin

Follow the road behind the seaside houses at Playa Quemada, heading towards Puerto Calero, then pick up a track running along the coast (see map pages 90-91). About 15 minutes before coming into Puerto Calero you must walk along the road. From Puerto Calero a footpath runs along the coast all the way back to Puerto del Carmen (at one point you have to take a detour above some villas to round the Barranco del Quiquere). Alternative walk 10-1 and Walk 8 follow this route.

FARO DE PECHIGUERA TO LA HOYA

Distance: 8km/5mi; under 3h

Grade: fairly easy

Transport: 🚌 (Timetable 5) or 🚗 to/from Playa Blanca, then 🚕 taxi to the Faro de Pechiguera to start. Return on 🚌 from La Hoya (Playa Blanca bus, Timetable 5)

From the lighthouse head north along the track shown on the touring map. (You can also walk along the coast if you like.) When you reach the abandoned *urbanización* Atlante del Sol (a large, isolated white building), you are just south of Walk 13. From here you can follow the track or the coastal path shown on the map on pages 104-105.

Coast at Orzola

Coastal path just east of the Barranco del Quiquere (Playa Quemada to Puerto del

PLAYA DE LA MADERA TO EL GOLFO

Distance: 13km/8mi; 5-6h
Grade: fairly strenuous if the whole walk is done, on account of the length; volcanic rock underfoot throughout (stout shoes essential)
Transport: 🚗 The best option is to ask friends to take you to the Playa de la Madera to start out, and to collect you at El Golfo. Alternatively, if you have a car, drive to Playa de la Madera and just follow the coastal path for as long as you like. *Note:* whether you are doing the entire walk or just part of it, it is better to start at Playa de la Madera, because there is *no* coastal path in the area just north of El Golfo.

*This is the only part of the Timanfaya National Park that you can explore without a guide, but you are asked **not** to venture off the made path.* The path leaves from the far side of the Playa de la Madera. The rock formations and the constant breaking of the waves are an endless source of enjoyment, and you have the backdrop of Timanfaya all along the route (photograph page 78). Just before the Playa del Paso you must pick up a track and follow it to the El Golfo road (there is no ongoing coastal path). Do **not** try to walk cross-country over the lava.

Coastal path north of the Salinas de Janubio

17 AROUND LOBOS

Distance: 10km/6.2mi; 2h45min

Grade: easy, but there is no shade, and it can be hot, windy and dusty.

Equipment: comfortable walking shoes, cardigan, sunhat, suncream, picnic, plenty of water, swimwear

How to get there and return: 🚢 from Playa Blanca to Lobos (at time of writing only three times a week: enquire on 517678 or ask at the port at Playa Blanca). Otherwise, 🚢 from Corralejo on Fuerteventura to Lobos (daily sailings from the port at 10.00; returns at 16.00)

You can have Fuerteventura's Jandía and El Jable; I'll settle for Lobos any day. A short — and not too rough — boat ride with an amiable seafarer takes you over to this strange little island of sand and rocky mounds. Seen from afar, it may not even arouse your curiosity. But once you've seen the exquisite lagoon cradled by Casas El Puertito and you've climbed the crater, then finished your day with a dip in the turquoise green waters off the shore, you'll remember it as one of the highlights of your holiday. Lobos takes its name from the seals that once inhabited these waters.

We follow a track that circles the 6.5km square island. Straight off the jetty, **start out** by taking the right-hand fork and head for the tiny port of Casas El Puertito, a few minutes away. A neat wide path leads us through a landscape dominated by mounds of lava and littered with rock. These small mounds, called *hornitos* ('little ovens'; see pages 120-121) are caused by phreatic eruptions. You'll see the beautiful *Limonium papillatum,* with its paper-like mauve and white flowers. And fluorescent green *tabaiba* glows amidst the sombre rock. You'll also notice plenty of *cosco (Mesembryanthemum nodiflorum),* the noticeably bright red ice plant, and *Suaeda vera.*

A reef of rocky outcrops shelters the lagoon, making it into a perfect natural swimming pool. Through the rock you can see the sand dunes of Corralejo in the background; this is a picture postcard setting. Emerging from the little houses, we continue around the lagoon. Almost at once, swing back inland and come to a T-junction: keep left here. *Arthrocnemum fruticosum* (a fern-like plant) grows in the hollows. Ice plants (see page 47), with their transparent papillae resembling drops of water, may also catch your attention. This plant was once traded for its soda content. The track loops its way through these miniature 'mountains'. Small sandy depressions lie ensconced amidst them. The rock is clad in orange and faded-green lichen. Overlooking all this is Montaña

Lobos (the crater), the most prominent feature in this natural park.

Shortly, cross a sandy flat area. The track forks; the right-hand fork becomes a path and cuts off a couple of corners; it rejoins the main route on the top of an embankment. Lanzarote begins to grow across the horizon. Ignore the forks off to the right at about **25min** and **30min** into the walk. The second fork leads past a patch of sisal — an aloe-like plant with exceptionally tall flower stems, sheltering in a hollow just a few minutes away. Close on **45min** into the walk, you come to a faint T-junction. Head left and, minutes further along, join a track coming in from the left, just below the lighthouse. Then climb up to it on a paved walkway. In a few minutes you're alongside the abandoned building and its outhouses. If you don't intend to climb the crater, this will be your best viewpoint in the walk. You look out over the dark lava hills and the tiny valleys of golden sand that thread their way through them. To the right of the broken-away crater of Montaña Lobos you'll glimpse Corralejo. Across the straits, just opposite, lie Lanzarote's magnificent beaches — stretching from Playa Blanca to Punta Papagayo.

From the lighthouse we follow the main track off to the right, into a manicured landscape. Just under 25 minutes from the lighthouse (at about **1h20min**), we turn off to climb Montaña Lobos. Take the first (faint) fork-off you come to, on your right. Straight into this track, the route forks. Go right and, some 120 paces along this fading fork, head straight off across the stones, aiming for the path that ascends the crater. Within a few minutes, cross a sandy hollow and reach the rim of the crater at about **1h40min**.

A brilliant sight awaits you. You find yourself on a razor-sharp ridge, looking down sheer walls onto a beach, hidden inside this half-crater. Your vista encompasses the profusion of *hornitos* that make up this island, the dunes of Corralejo, and Fuerteventura's hazy inland hills. To the north, you can see all along the coastline of Lanzarote as far as Puerto del Carmen.

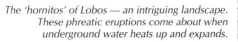

The 'hornitos' of Lobos — an intriguing landscape. These phreatic eruptions come about when underground water heats up and expands.

LOBOS

Punta Martino

Faro de Lobos

Caleta del Palo

Montaña Lobos
127

Caldera de la Montaña

Â
N

0 ___ 1 km
1/2 mi

Copyright © Sunflower Books

P

Playa de la Calera

P

Casas El Puertito

Caleta de la Rasca

Returning to the main track, head right. Barely 15 minutes after joining the track, we pass behind the main beach without even noticing it: the turn-off to it lies a few minutes beyond a fisherman's cottage that sits in a hollow on your left. This exquisite bay is actually a shallow lagoon that curves back deeply into the coastline. Here's where you'll end up passing the rest of the day, no doubt. Don't forget that the boat leaves at 4pm! To return to the ferry, just continue along the track (**2h45min**).

BUS TIMETABLES

1: Arrecife — Costa Teguise (Line 1); journey time 20min

Departures from Arrecife (Playa del Reducto)

Mondays to Fridays
06.45, 07.30, 08.10, 08.40, 09.10, 09.40, 10.10, 10.40, 11.10,
11.40, 12.10, 12.40, 13.10, 13.40, 14.10, 14.40, 15.10, 15.40,
16.10, 16.40, 17.10, 17.40, 18.10, 18.40, 19.10, 19.40, 20.10,
20.40, 21.10, 23.40

Saturdays, Sundays, holidays
06.40, 07.40, 08.40, 09.40, 10.40, 11.40, 12.40, 13.40, 14.40,
15.40, 16.40, 17.40, 18.40, 19.40, 20.40, 23.40

Departures from Costa Teguise*

Mondays to Fridays
07.15, 08.00, 08.30, 09.00, 09.30, 10.00, 10.30, 11.00, 11.30,
12.00, 12.30, 13.00, 13.30, 14.00, 14.30, 15.00, 15.30, 16.00,
16.30, 17.00, 17.30, 18.00, 18.30, 19.00, 19.30, 20.00, 20.30,
21.00, 23.30, 00.10

Saturdays, Sundays, holidays
07.00, 08.00, 09.00, 10.00, 11.00, 12.00, 13.00, 14.00, 15.00,
16.00, 17.00, 18.00, 19.00, 20.00, 21.00, 00.10

*All buses carry on to Puerto del Carmen, except for those underlined

2: Arrecife — Puerto del Carmen (Line 2); journey time 30min

Departures from Arrecife (Playa del Reducto)

Mondays to Fridays
06.20, 06.50, 07.20, 07.50, 08.20, 08.50, 09.20, 09.50, 10.20,
10.50, 11.20, 11.50, 12.20, 12.50, 13.20, 13.50, 14.20, 14.50,
15.20, 15.50, 16.20, 16.50, 17.20, 17.50, 18.20, 18.50, 19.20,
19.50, 20.20, 20.50, 21.20, 21.50, 22.30, 23.15

Saturdays
06.30, 07.20, 08.20, 09.20, 10.00, 10.20, 11.00, 11.20, 12.00,
12.20, 13.20, 14.00, 14.20, 15.00, 15.20, 16.00, 16.20, 17.20,
18.20, 19.20, 20.20, 21.20, 22.30, 23.15

Sundays, holidays
06.30, 07.20, 08.20, 09.20, 10.20, 11.20, 12.20, 13.20, 14.20,
15.20, 16.20, 17.20, 18.20, 19.20, 20.20, 21.20, 22.20, 23.15

Departures from Puerto del Carmen*

Mondays to Fridays
07.00, 07.30, 08.00, 08.30, 09.00, 09.30, 10.00, 10.30, 11.00,
11.30, 12.00, 12.30, 13.00, 13.30, 14.00, 14.30, 15.00, 15.30,
16.00, 16.30, 17.00, 17.30, 18.00, 18.30, 19.00, 19.30, 20.00,
20.30, 21.00, 21.30, 21.45, 22.00, 22.30, 00.00

Saturdays
07.00, 08.00, 09.00, 10.00, 10.30, 11.00, 11.30, 12.00, 12.30,
13.00, 14.00, 14.30, 15.00, 15.30, 16.00, 16.30, 17.00, 18.00,
19.00, 20.00, 21.00, 22.00, 23.00, 00.00

Sundays, holidays
07.00, 08.00, 09.00, 10.00, 11.00, 12.00, 13.00, 14.00, 15.00,
16.00, 17.00, 18.00, 19.00, 20.00, 21.00, 22.00, 23.00, 00.00

*All buses carry on to Costa Teguise, except for those underlined

3: Arrecife — airport — Playa Honda (Line 4); journey time 20min

Departures from Arrecife*

Mondays to Fridays
07.00, 08.10, 08.40, 09.10, 09.40, 10.10, 12.10, 12.40, 13.10,
14.40, 15.10, 15.40, 16.10, 16.40, 17.10, 18.10, 18.40, 19.10

Saturdays, Sundays, holidays
08.10, 08.40, 09.10, 09.40, 12.40, 13.10, 13.40, 14.10, 14.40,
15.10, 15.40, 16.10, 16.40, 17.10, 17.40

Departures from the airport

Mondays to Fridays
08.20, 08.50, 09.20, 09.50, 10.20, 12.20, 12.50, 13.20, 14.20,
15.20, 15.50, 16.20, 16.50, 17.20, 18.20, 18.50, 19.20

Saturdays, Sundays, holidays
08.20, 08.50, 09.20, 09.50, 12.50, 13.20, 13.50, 14.20, 14.50,
15.20, 15.50, 16.20, 16.50, 17.20, 17.50

*Underlined departures do *not* call at the airport

4: Arrecife — Femés — Conil — Asomada (Line 5); journey time to Femés approximately 1h

Departures from Arrecife

Mondays to Fridays only
14.00

Departures from Asomada

Mondays to Fridays only
07.00

5: Arrecife — Tías — Pto del Carmen — Playa Blanca (Line 6); journey time to Playa Blanca 1h10min

Departures from Arrecife

Mondays to Fridays
06.00, 08.00, 11.30, 14.00, 17.30, 20.15

Saturdays
07.00, 11.00, 13.30, 18.30

Sundays, holidays
08.00, 13.30, 18.30

Departures from Playa Blanca

Mondays to Fridays
06.50, 09.10, 12.40, 15.10, 18.40, 21.15

Saturdays
08.10, 12.10, 14.40, 19.40

Sundays, holidays
09.10, 14.40, 19.40

6: Arrecife — Arrieta — Haría — Máguez (Line 7)*; journey time to Máguez 1h05min

Departures from Arrecife

Mondays to Fridays
11.45, 14.00, 18.00, 20.00

Saturdays
11.00, 11.30, 20.00

Sundays, holidays
07.30, 13.30, 20.00

*Sometimes goes on to/returns from Ye; enquire in advance

continues overleaf

Departures from Máguez

Mondays to Fridays
07.00, 12.45, 16.00, 19.00
Saturdays
07.30, 12.00, 19.00
Sundays, holidays
08.45, 19.00

7: Arrecife — Teguise (Line 7); journey time 20min
Departures from Arrecife

Mondays to Fridays
07.40, 11.45, 14.00, 15.30, 18.00, 19.00, 20.00
Saturdays
07.40, 11.00, 13.30, 15.30, 20.00
Sundays, holidays
07.40, 08.00, 13.30, 15.30, 20.00

Departures from Teguise

Mondays to Fridays
07.05, 07.30, 09.00, 13.15, 15.50, 16.30, 17.00, 19.30
Saturdays
08.00, 09.00, 12.30, 17.00, 19.30
Sundays, holidays
09.00, 09.15, 17.00, 19.30

8: Arrecife — Orzola (Line 9); journey time 45min
Departures from Arrecife

Mondays to Fridays
07.40, 15.30
Saturdays, Sundays, holidays
07.40, 15.30

Departures from Orzola

Mondays to Fridays
08.30, 16.30
Saturdays, Sundays, holidays
08.30, 16.30

9: Arrecife — Los Valles (Line 10); journey time 30min
Departures from Arrecife

Mondays to Fridays only
14.00, 19.00

Departures from Los Valles

Mondays to Fridays only
07.00, 15.45

10: Arrecife — Güime — Montaña Blanca — San Bartolomé (Line 14); journey time 40min

Departures from Arrecife

Mondays to Fridays only
17.00, 13.30

Departures from San Bartolomé

Mondays to Fridays only
07.40, 14.00

11: Arrecife — San Bartolomé — Tiagua — Tinajo (Line 15); journey time to Tinajo 25min

Departures from Arrecife*

Mondays to Fridays
06.15, 08.00, 11.45, <u>13.40</u>, 14.00, 18.00, 20.00
Saturdays
08.00, 11.00, 13.30, 20.00
Sundays, holidays
07.45, 13.30, 20.00
*The underlined bus terminates at San Bartolomé

Departures from Tinajo

Mondays to Fridays
05.30, 07.15, 08.15, 09.00, 13.00, 15.45, 19.00
Saturdays
07.15, 08.45, 12.00, 19.00
Sundays, holidays
07.30, 08.30, 19.00

12: Arrecife — La Santa (Line 16); journey time about 1h

Departures from Arrecife

Mondays to Fridays only
08.00, 11.45, 14.00, 20.00

Departures from La Santa

Mondays to Fridays only
07.00, 08.45, 12.45, 18.45

13: Arrecife — Sóo (Line 17); journey time about 1h

Departures from Arrecife

Mondays to Fridays on ly
14.00, 19.00

Departures from Sóo

Mondays to Fridays only
07.10, 17.00

14: Arrecife — La Caleta (Line 18); journey time about 1h

Departures from Arrecife	**Departures from La Caleta**
Mondays to Fridays only	*Mondays to Fridays only*
14.00	07.00

The Volcan de Tindaya, the smaller of the two ferries plying between Lanzarote and Fuerteventura, leaving Corralejo

FERRY TIMETABLES

15: Buganvilla (Fred Olsen Line) from Playa Blanca* to Corralejo on Fuerteventura; journey time 40min
Departures from Playa Blanca
Daily
08.00, 10.00, 14.00, 18.00
Departures from Corralejo
Daily
09.00, 11.00, 17.00, 19.00
*A bus service departs Puerto del Carmen (Muelle del Varadero) daily at 09.00 and 17.00, to connect with the 10.00 and 18.00 sailings. On the return, buses will meet the 09.00 and 17.00 sailings from Fuerteventura.

16: Volcan de Tindaya (Armas Line) from Playa Blanca to Corralejo on Fuerteventura; journey time 40min
Departures from Playa Blanca
Daily
09.00, 11.00, 17.00, 19.00
Departures from Corralejo
Daily
18.00, 10.00, 14.00, 18.00

17: Graciosa Ferry (from Orzola); journey time 25min
Departures from Orzola
Daily
10.00, 12.00, 17.00 (and 18.30 in summer)
Departures from Caleta del Sebo (Graciosa)
Daily
09.00, 11.00, 16.00 (and 18.00 in summer)

Index

Geographical names comprise the only entries in this index; for other entries see Contents, page 3. **Bold-face type** indicates a photograph; *italic type* indicates a map reference. Both may be in addition to a text reference on the same page.